Sybil Skakle grew up in my favorth Carolina Outer Banks. Her new m ....f the Shadow, an account of Sybil's life a ....of 33 years. What Came Next tells of her q........ ....

She explores the changing culture associated with dating and intimacy in the new millennium and must choose between the values and beliefs of her youth and those of the hook-up culture.

She marries Sir Charles on the rebound. Five years later, Sir Charles leaves. In her desperate search for companionship, she chooses the unlikely Cowpoke, a man she has corresponded with, but never met. She visits him. Torn between two loves and God's love, she tries to solve the problem without hurting either of the men or compromising her moral beliefs.

After divorcing Sir Charles, she cannot make up her mind whether to pursue her writing career or to marry Cowpoke, who is dying. Due to her compassion she compromises and marries him. He wanted to go to Hawaii for their honeymoon. His oncologist advised him to go, in effect it was now or never for him. They went. Their trip was cut short by his illness.

On top of all this she has to fight for her inheritance consisting of Hatteras Island property left by her father to her brothers and sisters. To prove their claim Sybil tracks the history of the land to the original land grants of Hatteras Banks in 1711-1712.

This is a sad but well told story of a lovely, sensitive, intelligent woman and her quest for love after her first husband, the love of her life, went home to Heaven. He left her alone and bereft of that sweet companionship and the intimacy she shared with him.

—E. B. Alston
Publisher and Editor in Chief for *Righter Monthly Review*

What Came Next is an honest and touching memoir of a woman's struggles and triumphs. Mrs. Skakle is most engaging as love, family and values collide to test her faith. This memoir is a must share life lesson as Mrs. Skakle shares her tenacity to overcome personal adversity without losing her faith.

—Mavi Sanchez

Sybil Skakle's story is a good read, full of lessons learned as her new life unfolds. Her experience, similar to ours, can benefit her readers.

—Rev. Nancy Sturdivant, UMC

What Came Next

The Story of a Widow's Loves and Life After Loss

SYBIL AUSTIN SKAKLE

WESTBOW
PRESS
A DIVISION OF THOMAS NELSON
& ZONDERVAN

Scripture taken from the King James Version of the Bible.

WestBow Press books may be ordered through booksellers or by contacting:

WestBow Press
A Division of Thomas Nelson & Zondervan
1663 Liberty Drive
Bloomington, IN 47403
www.westbowpress.com
1 (866) 928-1240

ISBN: 978-1-4908-2780-3 (sc)
ISBN: 978-1-4908-2781-0 (e)

Library of Congress Control Number: 2014903575

Printed in the United States of America.

WestBow Press rev. date: 04/11/2014

CHAPTER

1

After the sudden, unexpected death of my husband Don in 1980, I lived in shadow valley for many months. The title of my memoir about that time is *Valley of the Shadow--a journey through grief,* copyright 2009, IUniverse. During the valley sojourn, I experienced denial, anger, regret, guilt, and, finally, acceptance. With the help of friends and a psychiatrist, I learned many things I needed to know to ford rivers successfully, traverse mountains and survive the deserts of the fifth decade of a lone woman's life. I once expressed regret to my psychiatrist that activities and work took me away from Don when talking to me might have reduced the stress, which I believed caused his death. Dr. Somers said, "Your being there does not mean he would have talked. There were times when you were there when he could have talked and didn't."

Nevertheless, I felt that it must have been a lack in me that prevented him from sharing his feelings readily. I also felt that, if I had been a better mother, our middle son Andy's second marriage would not have failed. Dr. Somers and Andy had a doctor/patient relationship too. I talked to Dr. Somers about my concerns related to Andy. During one visit, Dr. Somers shook his head and said, "Good old mother!"

"You think I am too responsible!" I said, and he nodded his head in agreement.

This following story occurs between 1982 and 1992, as I confront life's difficulties without the support of a parent or a spouse. It reminds me of John Bunyan's *Pilgrim's Progress,* written in 1678, which was an allegorical story of a person's struggles on the journey to Celestial City. I hope to arrive there too and finally to understand all the mysteries of life, including why I could not keep my loved ones safe. Bunyan and I are separated by hundreds of years but his characters and I share the same hope, which is in the person of Christ Jesus, the Son of God.

By 1982, with the answers I had found, I felt ready to move forward. My hospital pharmacist position provided financial security, as well as a reason for getting up each day. It enabled me to care for myself and would enable me to help one or the other of our three grown sons during the recession of the early '80s with shelter or shillings.

My employment provided opportunities to meet and interact with people. I liked and respected those with whom I worked. I had friends and acquaintances outside the workplace. I belonged to professional groups, played active leadership roles in my local church, and attended writing and poetry groups. I was a fortunate woman. I was restless and lonely, dissatisfied with my life without Don. I valued my matchless female friendships, but without male companionship, which differs mysteriously, I felt incomplete. The magnetism, evident early and lasting a lifetime, between male and female is true for most of us. "God created them male and female" (Genesis 1:27).

My story begins.

Olga, a close friend and neighbor, a smart businesswoman, and I were having tea in my yellow kitchen one day in 1982. Don and I depended on her to do our taxes for several years and, after his death, she guided me through the probate of his estate. She had been a woman alone for many years and knew the single territory. She understood my feeling and I could trust her.

She told me about Single Book Lovers, an organization begun in 1970 to help men and women meet through their interest in books. Their slogan: A Good Book is a Good Friend.

"You don't need to be lonely," Olga said. "You can meet fine men by writing letters."

Books are good friends. They provide company during hours alone, as well as topics for conversation with friends or strangers. Books might nurture new friendships, and reading and writing were and are favorite pastimes of mine. I have met many interesting characters from whom I have learned during my literary lifetime. I continue to learn from those I meet. People's stories help me grow and to understand personal relationships as much as personal networking itself does.

The Single Book Lovers' modest membership fee entitled me to receive three profiles monthly. I could buy additional ones for a nominal cost. The profile provided the candidate's family status, profession, vocation, and hobbies, as well as their height, weight, and color of eyes and hair. Each member explained in a short essay what he or she wanted of a relationship; and was encouraged to express religious and political views.

Single Book Lovers still exists. Its website contains the following statement: *SBL is a singles relationship group that posts personals of single, divorced, and widowed men and women. The common element among this group is the love of books, reading, arts, and culture.* These shared interests provide the basis for a relationship built on expectation of intellectual chemistry, I suppose. Their slogan reads: "If you know the books someone reads you know their friends."

Writing enabled me to express my creativity and humanity without challenge or contradiction. Writing belongs to the writer, while conversation belongs to both participants. I believed that I could express my ideas and feelings in writing better than by talking to someone, and this venture was somewhat like window-shopping. I did not have to buy. It gave me a chance to view the person with my mind and heart, without distraction and without commitment. While I remained safe in my own community with old friends, I could meet new ones by the means of membership in Single Book Lovers. In my introduction letter to those I chose, I wrote that I welcomed letters from anyone who cared to write, but had no interest in a physical relationship except under the authority and commitment of marriage.

Prior to his father's death, our son Andy, who had been teaching tennis in an Eastern North Carolina town, returned home, after his marriage failed and he lost the position. With no job prospects, one Saturday he was selling his possessions for spending money. Mary Sigrist, back "home" in Carrboro to be near her family after the death of her chef husband in Maryland, came to his yard sale for diversion. When I learned that she was mourning too, I invited her into my kitchen to share coffee and sympathy. This began a friendship that was to have great meaning for both of us.

Mary and I joined a couple of local singles groups, attended a few dances, and stood on the sidelines, feeling self-conscious and demeaned when we were ignored and no one asked us to dance. We joined a Christian group, sponsored by a husband and wife, whose first marriages had ended by divorce. During a Christmas party at their home, we enjoyed the relaxed, natural, exchange between single men and women. It was a great contrast to our experience at the single dances, when, standing on the sidelines, we were like monkeys at the zoo awaiting a treat.

Mary joined an international writing group of individuals in a higher-income bracket. She rented a post office box to protect her physical address and invited me to share it.

Soon I began to receive interesting letters and an occasional phone call. I first heard from Lee Paul Stanley in May of 1982. Since he had once sold pharmaceuticals and read in my profile that I was a pharmacist, he thought we had something in common. When I received his letter, I phoned him and liked the sound of his voice.

One day, on my way home from work and the grocery store, I picked up a letter from him at the post office. Lee wrote, "For the '80s, people in our age group don't need marriage. Maybe these young folks know more than we do. Why not just live together?"

Anxious to answer him, I came into the house and started the washing machine, intending to put the clothes lying on the floor into the machine. Instead, I sat down to write and let the washing machine run through a whole cycle without clothes. I forgot to bring the groceries in from the car!

Lee's liberal views bothered me and I considered ending our correspondence then and there. True, we would not be committing adultery and had no fear of producing our kind, but sex outside of marriage was still against God's law and society. I knew that passage in 1 Corinthians 6:9-10: "No fornicators ... shall inherit the kingdom of God."

Besides, life had already taught me that any willful disobedience to God's loving efforts to take care of me would have consequence in guilt and pain for me. I understood that correlation since I joined the church at 12 years of age. My Christian witness monitored my actions and behavior. My consideration of and responsibility to my sons, my unborn grandchildren, other family members, my church family, and the community at large were restraints. My deceased parents! My departed husband! Failure to practice moral standards I had taught my sons would be a betrayal and hypocrisy.

Our letters, between Chapel Hill, North Carolina, and Kansas City, Missouri, kept life interesting. He and I had been alone for similar lengths of time. Lee's second wife died in February 1979 and Don in April 1980. Sometimes Lee's letters were so specific about what he wanted: *"slender, five feet, six-inch woman with hips to fit size ten or twelve jeans."* I cringed! What made this overweight, over-short, sixty-plus male think he could make such demands? My hips needed a sixteen petite for a five feet, two and one-half inches tall figure. I detested "dungarees" and had not worn anything similar since a World War II date told me: "Sybil, your fly is open."

I like pants with no front opening and elastic in the waist. My ability to be a loving, interesting companion does not hinge on my wearing jeans or the size of my hips! The idea of trying to fit into some sexual fantasy angered and sickened me. I wrote and told him how I felt.

I had lofty ideas of our serving God together in some noble cause! My reason for supposing that possible was that he did not smoke, drink, or gamble. Then, he indicated that he thought I wanted to "swing" and I responded: "We are not on the same page!"

I had calls from other SBL men. A man from Connecticut actually discussed books in his interesting letters and visited another SBL woman in Raleigh. I was not disappointed that he did not visit me as planned. He talked of a physical relationship. He was too much younger than I to be a candidate for marriage. I heard from a retired United Methodist minister from Winston-Salem, whom I would meet later.

Lee urged me to come for a visit. "Western men always expect their women to come to them."

"Well, I am a Southern romantic, who expects an older version of Lochinvar to ride out of the west to claim my pledge of love," I answered. I wondered if this person, who signed his letters "Cowpoke" and claimed he liked to raise cows would qualify. Might I influence his thinking? Might my prayers, added to those of his 90-year-old Catholic mother, help God change his priorities? When I wrote and offered to be his friend instead of his lover, I may have been naïve. Perhaps he was treating me like a buddy when he told me about the other SBL women who came to visit him. Was he trying to make me green-eyed? Once he wrote, "I need to find a woman with at least five oil wells."

"Oh, I go to Hatteras and put on my mermaid outfit and dive for oysters. The activity is most lucrative. The oysters we harvest have pearls. Sorry, I should have told you! Pearls instead of oil wells!"

Verbal sparring with Lee was fun. By August 1982, we were exchanging several letters a week. Since SBL suggested we discuss books, I decided to discuss *The Passions of the Mind*, a biographical novel about the life of Sigmund Freud by Irving Stone that I was reading. "You and Freud agree that sex is the primal urge," I wrote.

By referring to Stone's book, I hoped to interest him beyond his expectation of attracting a beauty queen and to disqualify one of his remarks. "You say I do not admit that sex is important. Not true! According to Freud, the human mind is highly vulnerable. A sexual experience of an eighteen-month-old child caused a mental disturbance in his adulthood. Sex is definitely important!"

We shared concerns about our families, as we considered our lives and thoughts of independence from their demands on our lives. His daughter Barbara was anticipating divorce. My oldest son Eddie and his wife Kathey, married twelve years, were living in separate quarters. We imagined the reactions of our offspring. Could we withstand any objections they might have? Would their opinions influence our decisions? Our supposed obligations to our children hovered over our heads and around our hearts. My sons' seeming neglect of me sometimes troubled me, but my loyalty to them was a factor as I thought of making my own happiness first priority. Money and property were concerns for both of us. I wrote to Lee, "I belong to myself, not to the past, not to my heirs! Nor do they belong to me. What I have is mine. If I choose to give it to them, I may. I am not obligated."

My theory, while true, was untested. My sons were the ones who needed to hear and understand what I was saying to Lee.

Lee had written, "I don't think Barb would want me to marry."

Barbara, born of his first marriage, was self-supporting, worked at the University of Missouri and may have needed his emotional support at the time, as her five-year marriage ended. He helped her move into her own apartment when it happened. Lee's three grown stepchildren wanted him to sell the house and to divide the proceeds. "Where would I live? I have to live somewhere. If I decide to marry again, the house is all I have," he said.

Lee wrote that he belonged to a Kansas City writing group, so I wrote and told him about my plans to attend a Christian Writers' Conference in Black Mountain. "I'm going to come," he said, when we talked on the phone. "Why don't we room together?"

I dismissed his comment, thought he was teasing. However, the day I drove toward Black Mountain, with two older Christian friends, I suddenly felt a sense of panic. How would I explain Lee to my friends if he showed up at the conference?

Truthfully, my interest in Lee embarrassed me. Would people think me crazy for a man and disloyal to Don?

Florence, a vivacious, retired college professor from Western Carolina University, my roommate the year before, would have understood. She was older and had raised three daughters alone after her husband's early death. She would have understood, even have smiled at the poem I wrote to Lee.

My Fantasy

Motivated by imagination and desire
My restless heart began to plan
To dream of your great achievement
Of your recapturing old ideals
To live and serve God
Together with me
I longed to know the man you were-
The crusading editor
The potential pastor
Who you were before war
And the world made you cynical
Before grief left you sad.

Registration entitled each of us to an interview with an editor and one of us, Frances Bradsher, connected with a publisher at once, who bought her family memoir: *The Preacher Had Ten Kids.* As for me, I lacked self-confidence and dreaded asking anyone to look at my writing. When I finally met my interviewer, he needed to talk about the death of someone close to him. I listened, relieved by the distraction that kept us from discussing my writing.

There were no letters awaiting me from Lee at the post office, but two at the house. Neither letter had a post office box number, or an address. Postal automation, with installation of optical character readers, began in 1982. However, in Chapel Hill, human hands were still sorting the mail and someone who scanned these letters knew where I lived!

"I have a confession," I wrote Lee. "There were many vans at Black Mountain and I checked every license plate, ones from Kentucky, Florida, Tennessee, and other far places. There were none from Missouri."

"I didn't have the money to go to the conference," he said.

Two days after our return from Black Mountain, I received a letter from SBL Charles Andre Fetterroll of Nanuet, New York, who wrote that I already held second place. Am *I competing?* I wondered. I replied to see if I could achieve first place.

Still, Cowpoke and Carolina, the name Lee called me, kept up a lively exchange of letters. He called to talk about his mother's stroke and the twelve inches of rain, which flooded his basement, and told me that he had high blood pressure. I urged him to see a doctor.

At home, I had my own challenges! My psychiatrist advised me to "make verbal contracts" with two of my three grown sons to help me with household tasks. After a heated conversation one evening, I sat and listened while Cliff and Andy enumerated my limitations. Finally, one of them leveled the refrigerator and repaired the door on the stove. I had stood my ground and made a contract, but their displeasure spoiled my victory.

Late in August, I had letters from both Charles and Lee. Charles' seeming unashamed devotion to God elevated him in my opinion. We seemed to agree that marriage was the only foundation for a serious relationship. Would he be as human as Lee? Then, as I yearned for Don during a church worship service one Sunday, I felt chastened. Should I become involved with another man?

By the end of August, Charles' hand-decorated envelopes filled the rented post office box. He wrote that he planned to come to North Carolina the last week of September to visit his third ranked pen pal in Eden, North Carolina, and would like to visit me.

Still, I wanted to see Lee and, when I talked to him that evening, I told him, "All day today a song kept running through my mind: 'Don't Give up on Me Baby!'"

"Sweetie," he said, "I might break your heart."

"How do you know you will break my heart? Maybe I'll break yours. Are you willing to take a chance if I am?"

"Sweetie, it is a thousand miles to Chapel Hill from Kansas City. My arms can't reach that far," he said.

However, he visited relatives in Washington, Pennsylvania, renewed acquaintance with a woman he knew as a teenager, who had lost her physician husband to death. A spark ignited and he decided he loved Mary, whose economic position was closer to oil-well ownership than mine!

Nevertheless, we continued to correspond and when I told him that Charles was coming to visit, he asked me to send him a picture of us. "So I can see how you look together."

Obligingly, he sent me one of Mary and him, so I could see how they looked together. Did his request indicate more than curiosity? I decided to concentrate on the more willing suitor, but before that, Shirley Durham and I attended the Knoxville World's Fair that August. Its theme was "Energy in Motion." We learned what we might expect in the years ahead, but my mind wandered as we explored the exhibits. I wondered about Lee and about the New York SBL.

I dressed carefully for work the Saturday morning before Charles Fetterroll was due to arrive at Raleigh-Durham Airport from LaGuardia in late afternoon. Under my lab coat, I wore a light brown suit trimmed in beige and I wore heels instead of work shoes. As my workday ended, my nervousness mounted and further increased as I drove toward the airport.

His plane should have arrived when I got to the airport, so I parked at the curb and went inside. Even though we had exchanged photos, I was not sure I would recognize Charles and searched the face of every older man. As I stood in the middle of the waiting area, two men came out of the bar. The older one stopped in front of me. "Do I know you?" he asked.

"No, sir, I'm sure you do not." I said.

Amused by my discomfort, he smiled and turned away.

The lines of people from the incoming plane came around the corner and I spotted him. He recognized me, smiled broadly and came toward me with outstretched arms. Sweat covered his brow. I suspect that Sir Charles, arriving by plane instead of steed, was as unsure as his "Angel Sybil from the Southern Part of Heaven" was.

We retrieved his luggage, went outside. My car was gone! A porter volunteered, "It was towed."

Mortified, I asked, "How do I get it back?"

"You'll have to go over to the parking lot and claim it. It's going to cost you!"

"How do I get there?"

"That van will take you," said the red cap, with a flourish of his hand.

"We'll both go," Charles said. "I don't want to let you out of my sight!"

We found my tan 1980 Plymouth Horizon and I paid the penalty. We loaded Charles' luggage and headed toward Chapel Hill.

"I want to take you to a nice place for dinner," he said. "Where do you suggest?"

Slug's, once known as The Pines, on the east side of Chapel Hill, seemed more recommendable than Brady's on East Franklin Street. However, I liked Brady's oysters better than Slug's steak.

I drove Charles to The Carolina Inn, a Chapel Hill landmark since 1924, in the center of downtown Chapel Hill and on the edge of the University of North Carolina campus. An attendant led us up to the room they had reserved for Charles. This new role made me feel anxious and uncomfortable and I quickly escaped for home to dress and to think. I needed to recover my poise. Charles seemed too effusive, too cheerful. Since he was a guest of sorts, I needed to be kind and to withhold judgment. Perhaps anxiety made him chatter so.

When I returned to the inn, he proudly presented to me a sonnet he had written in my absence. My guest was full of surprises!

Our hostess at Slug's seated us far back near the kitchen door. When Charles immediately assessed the traffic problem and requested new seating, I was grateful and impressed.

During dinner, this man from New York, the father of seven children, confided that he was a heart attack survivor. Slightly stunned, I concluded that life is always uncertain. Recently, I had read of a groom killed on couple's honeymoon. We do not know how long we will live. We dare! We risk! Only by risking, do we really live. Today is between yesterday and forever.

Charles explored Chapel Hill while I worked. On Wednesday night, my friends Mary and Jim took him with them to the Billy Graham Crusade in Kenan Memorial Stadium. They planned to check him out for me. That night after the crusade, Charles hired a taxi to take him to Durham, eight miles or so away, to ride home with me from work. The taxi driver took him to Duke Hospital instead of Durham General. I was on my way home before he arrived at Durham General. He seemed highly amused by his misadventure. Gracious! What unexpected behavior!

Following a 10-day stretch, my weekend began Thursday morning. After breakfast, we drove to Durham to see Duke University campus. We visited Duke Chapel and walked through Duke Gardens. I asked someone we met to take a picture of us, so I could send a copy to Lee. I took Charles to see the Duke Homestead and Tobacco Museum on our way to North Durham to visit the Eno River State Park. We walked around the grounds and while we sat in the sunshine at a picnic table, sharing our histories and expectations, he suddenly declared his love for me and asked me to marry him.

It was September. We had been writing since July. While I wanted to believe I was interesting and attractive, I doubted that he could be sure of love so quickly. Besides, earlier while we were at the Sarah Duke Gardens, he said he still loved Julie, whom he had married after his wife Mildred died of a stroke at forty-something.

His marriage to Julie, the widow of a friend of his, and the mother of a son and a daughter, had been stormy. He thought the rivalry between their children complicated their ten-year marriage. When things got too tense, Julie retired to the home she retained on Long Island with her two children, leaving Charles and his two youngest children at the new home, which he claimed he built for her; and gave her in the divorce settlement.

Then, he married Pat, a psychiatric nurse, a SBL from Oregon, or Washington State. From his account, their marriage, though short, had been good and strengthened his relationships with his children. Childless, Pat appreciated being part of Charles' family. Charles explained that Pat's former marriage had been abusive and that she thanked him for theirs. I thought of his life before she came and whispered, "Bless Pat!"

Both he and Pat were in the hospital when he had the heart attack. He recovered enough to go home, but Pat died. I do not know how long their marriage had been. Still, he spoke of Julie as the one he would always love! I thought that he might still have issues to solve before marrying anyone, especially me! I do not play second fiddle! Later he qualified his remark to make it more palatable. Christianity teaches that we are to love others. Greeks have four names for love. *Of course, agape!* He could love Julie without being "in love" with Julie!

I had declared my motherly independence, but I invited Andy and Cliff to have dinner with Charles and me. In spite of how they may have felt, they were courteous and did their part to make the evening a success. They did their father and me proud.

Cliff had still lacked a few credits when he took off on the tennis circuit. On the eve of the United States National Tennis Championships in New York the year before, Cliff defended a karate kick his doubles partner threw and it resulted in a broken right wrist. While his wrist healed, he went to Hawaii to live and to work for several months with a college friend before he returned and sought to regain his tennis ranking. When that failed, he enrolled at Carolina to complete his degree in physical education and graduated with the cap and gown ceremony early May 1983!

Saturday arrived and I packed a lunch for a picnic somewhere along our way to visit my sisters Margie, in Greensboro, and Mona, in Winston-Salem. My oldest sister Margie and her husband Curtis were gracious, as they always were. After a short visit with them, my car stopped on I-40 just beyond Greensboro. We left my car at the nearby service station for repairs and walked to the airport, which was within walking distance. There Charles rented a red Cavalier Chevrolet. He responded to the inconvenience and hassle in a positive way for our first crisis and I gave him the grade of A for his performance under pressure.

We abandoned our picnic plans and drove to Winston-Salem to see my youngest sister Mona and her new husband, Bill Hunter, married May 1982. Mona's facial expression registered her misgivings when she met my new suitor. Mona and Bill had plans for the evening, so we chatted with them while we ate our picnic lunch on their kitchen table and then left to return to Chapel Hill.

There were curious glances from my church friends when I walked into Amity United Methodist Church Sunday morning with a tall stranger. Some friends, already alerted, were interested and came forward to meet the creator of the colorful envelopes I had been receiving. Sir Charles met the test that morning.

Monday, I drove Andy's car to guide Charles halfway to the airport, before turning back to drive to work. Charles returned the rental at the airport. Andy found someone to take him to Greensboro to pick up my car the next day.

With Charles gone, I turned my attention to my own activities, which included a pharmacy seminar at the Research Triangle. Now that the novelty of his visit was over, I had things to consider. On impulse, I called Lee to tell him about Charles' visit. Lee's voice was pleasant and soothing to my ear. "Are you going to marry him?" he asked.

"I don't know about that, but he asked me."

"Do you love him?"

"I don't know."

How could I possibly know if I loved Charles? I studied Don for thirty-four and one-half years. Charles, almost as tall, walked and talked differently. Certainly, I knew not to expect anyone to be like Don. Every person is unique. Every snowflake has a shape all its own! I had reservations about Charles.

My nurse friend Jo Hudson (Lowdermilk) at the hospital and I often ate lunch together. She and I struggled with similar questions as we adjusted to widowhood. We were able to share honestly and freely. Once I told Jo, "If I ever meet someone I want to marry, he has to smell right."

Charles did not exactly smell bad. Perhaps the oily, metallic odor of his clothing was due to his work. Soap and water would take care of his clothing. I knew how to wash clothes. Surely, I should not reject the man because his clothes smelled odd. Not dirty, just odd! Would Lee smell right?

Charles said that he liked competition. "Go ahead and date others," he said. "The sooner you decide the better!"

I invited the retired United Methodist minister from Winston-Salem to attend a football game with me. We talked easily. Divorced, he blamed his wife's mental illness for her divorcing him. When his bishop asked him to leave the church, he felt doubly rejected. I suspected he still loved Sue, the mother of his son and daughter. Another evening, he responded to my impromptu invitation to play bridge in Chapel Hill. The next time I visited Mona and Bill, we invited the clergyman for a fourth for bridge. We were a congenial group. I had good cards. "Sybil, do you pray for those cards?" he asked and laughed.

Mona sent me an observation: "If the You that is You and the I that is I do not agree, then WE cannot be."

Time would tell whether Charles and I were to be, or, if there would be another more agreeable for me.

CHAPTER

3

My intent to see Charles in his environment and meet his family seemed a rational decision if I was to consider marrying him. When I first broached the subject, Charles seemed reluctant to have me come. Two weeks later, he suggested I plan to come during my next four-day break. Instead of going to Hatteras as planned, I would drive to Virginia Beach to spend the night with my niece Beth Williams, and would fly from Norfolk International Airport to New York La Guardia. I would be able to drive to visit Eddie at Hatteras from Virginia Beach afterward.

My sons did not comment, but they may have been aghast that I thought to visit a man, as far away as New York City, whom I had known less than six months. Maybe I was the only one who thought my actions astonishing. If other women I knew did things like this, they kept it secret from me. My friends seemed to live safely within convention, while the younger generation adventured.

An adventurous child, I had tested myself against the waves and the deep of the Atlantic Ocean. My trip to New York was rather like risks I took when I ventured out to the reefs, beyond the deep water. Sometimes in getting back to shore, the current of the surf tumbled and swept me along the bottom of the ocean so that I felt I would surely drown before I could get my feet back under me. I had felt threatened at times during my adulthood, but this was not one of them.

Charles met me at the airport and then drove to Nanuet and to the motel, across the street from his apartment. I rested and freshened up while he went to do the same. He returned, wearing a felt hat and had red handkerchief in his pocket. He looked very nice. Then why was I surprised?

Over dinner, at a nice Chinese restaurant, we shared our expectations. We both voiced a desire for more personal time, after having spent years of employment and being responsible for our families. Our grown children needed to be responsible for their own affairs. We agreed that in a marriage the spousal relationship should be of first importance.

When he picked me up next morning to go to Upstate New York to see other family, he had bags of bagels and cream cheese to take to each family group. We had a bagel with coffee for breakfast and were on our way. I enjoyed the scenery and observed a tall nuclear plant tower against the sky as we traveled north. His four sons and one daughter lived in Middle Grove, which is near the tourist resort of Saratoga Springs, known for its famous mineral water and horse race tracks.

Our first visit was to Charles' oldest son Robert and wife, Susan, where I held their new baby, dressed in a very small turtleneck with jeans, to have a picture taken. At his daughter Jean's house, his son Willie, a bachelor who lived nearby in a trailer, had erected a slab of wood he had inscribed: **Sybil and Charles**. Willie, Jean, her two children, Paul and Doobie (Jean Marie) from an earlier marriage, her husband Dave and their small daughter Rebecca, greeted us.

Jean's home had been the family's vacation home. According to Charles, Millie, his wife and the mother of his children, managed to buy 100 acres of land, from their earnings. Millie had babies and worked for the New York City underground transportation system, while Charles sometimes held two jobs. Millie's dream had been to have the family move upstate to start a business, which would provide for all of them. Their living quarters reminded me of my own early life at Hatteras. There was no running water. They brought water in a bucket to the house from a stream down the hill. It surprised me that anyone, even in rural New York, was without bathroom facilities by 1982. These young folks were struggling to stay alive, yet their hospitality warmed my heart.

Before we started back to Nanuet, we visited his two other bachelor sons, Charles and Paul. Veronica, the oldest child, a victim of schizophrenia, lived in a village or town near Nanuet. I did not meet her at the time, but would meet the youngest, his daughter Lorrell, before I left New York.

By the time we arrived back to Nanuet, around nine o'clock that night, we were weary and ready to be in bed, so we said our goodnights.

Next morning, I checked out of the motel and we ate a simple breakfast at his apartment. When we opened the door to go to the airport, Lorrell stood there. She would go to visit her grandmother and to the airport with us. Before our visit to her grandmother's apartment, near La Guardia, we ate lunch.

Charles' mother, Louise Fetterroll, a handsome 90-year-old woman, greeted us. She still cared about her appearance. Her hair was dyed dark brown and she was attractively dressed. Andre, Charles' middle name, is French and was Louise's family

21

name. Fetterroll is German. Her small, pleasant, nicely furnished apartment, located on an upper floor, was in a protected building.

Louise had been a garment maker in New York City. Charles expressed his pride in his mother's abilities. He told me about the beautiful dresses she designed for his sister Mildred to wear when, as young adults, he escorted her to the dances at Roseland. Their mother and father separated early in their lives. (Mildred now lives in Rapid City, South Dakota, with her husband Ray.)

Louise greeted us cheerfully from her wheelchair, asked about his family and was pleased to see Lorrell. When she asked about Ronnie, the name they call Veronica, Charles became agitated, perhaps because we had failed to see her.

When they called for boarding at the airport, I had failed to pick up my boarding pass. It was too late. I missed my eight o'clock departure, and had no chance to call Beth. Instead, I dashed for the shuttle, in pouring rain, to be transported to another terminal to take the express flight to Norfolk. Beth had been waiting for me since before nine and my plane arrived at eleven. The New York storm had affected Norfolk and Hatteras, as well. Trees were down in the Norfolk area and tides had eroded the Hatteras Island beaches.

I spent a couple of days at Hatteras and, back home again, I was able to review my experience. Charles wanted to buy me a ring while I was in New York. I was not ready. He gave me two figurines, a young boy with a white cap and blue knickers and a blonde-haired dancing girl in a red costume. He said, "When you have decided, put them together and then tell me."

His world was so different from mine. Would it work for us? His seven children represented a threat, especially the schizoid one. I had enough conflicts with my own offspring and their problems, which I wanted to escape. I needed someone to help me face my life. It awed me to think of relating to ten individuals, his offspring and mine. Would they expect me to mother them? Would I expect it of myself?

Most of the people in the small community where I lived as a little girl were my relatives. Both parents' families had been part of America since before the Revolutionary War. My life was stable with a mother and a father. Charles was born and raised in New York City, a first generation American on his father's side of the family. His parents separated early in his life, but were never divorced, and Charles blamed his mother for depriving him of his father. Yet, he sought to please her and feared her displeasure.

Another question concerned Evelyn, a local woman Charles told me he dated sometimes. I decided she must have been the number one contender for his affection. He explained that he needed to "let her down easy." I suspected she was the reason he hesitated to have me visit!

Would the difference in our work category be a problem? Prototype machinist is an honorable profession that requires intelligence and creativity. My pharmacist position may have greater status, but I believe that interdependence on all work makes all categories of equal value and importance to God and to society, and to me as an individual!

I wondered if I were overly romantic to think God put Charles into my life. Maybe it was my desire for an escape from my own problems and loneliness.

Lee called, talked about Mary Jane, the woman in Pennsylvania. He thought she could handle her alcoholism except for her son. He asked, "Did you marry the New Yorker?"

CHAPTER 4

One night in November, during a series of services at my church, reminiscent of the traditional revivals of the past, a visiting minister said, "Anything God leads you to, if it is not right for you, the Holy Spirit will lead you out of it."

That seemed like my confirmation to me. I came home and called Charles. "The little boy in blue trousers and the dancing girl are together. Charles, I will marry you."

The pharmacy department planned a Thanksgiving party and I impulsively phoned Charles and asked if he would like to come. There was no hesitation. "Yes!!"

There were curious smiles when I brought him to the party.

I had invited Charles to stay at my home. By now, Andy and Cliff were living elsewhere, but I did not think I needed a chaperone. He retired before I did that night. I peeked into his room on my way to bed. He was asleep, but had turned down the covers as though he expected me to join him.

While he was here, we shopped for a diamond for me and he voiced a plan for an engagement dinner in Saratoga Springs with his family, sometime in January, to announce our engagement and to share our joys.

Before that weekend, there were the pre-Christmas activities at church to keep me occupied. I did my usual stint at the Amity Christmas tree sales and sang the lovely cantata with the church choir. Both Charles and I were having doubts and expressed them to the other. He said, "You are like a hot air balloon about to go off into the ether."

"I do make great demands of myself," I said. "When I see others doing their part, I want to do mine!"

Could Charles be my ballast? Would he want to be? Would I allow him to be?

Eddie and Kathey came for Christmas, even though they were getting a divorce. Andy, Cliff and they, and I were nostalgic as we talked of other Christmases and we missed Don, their father.

Charles and I quarreled over the phone one night. Our conversation was relaxed and pleasant the next night. Our emotional and psychological problems drained my energies and caused me to worry more. What lessons would God teach us?

In early January 1983, Eddie and Kathey's divorce became final. I blamed Eddie, but Kathey said, "That's not fair! We were both at fault. When one was ready to cooperate, the other was contrary."

The time came for me to go to New York for our engagement event. I arrived at La Guardia, but Charles was not there. While I waited, a man sitting next to me engaged me in conversation. He opened a paper bag at his feet, extracted some albums, and showed me newspaper clippings concerning a court case he argued and won. When I told him that I was a writer, he invited me to come and be a guest on his TV show. I doubted his claims and thought him an eccentric, but he chattered on, "Why do you suppose you are waiting here?" he asked.

"I am waiting for my fiancé," I said. "I've called his apartment. He must be on his way."

"No! It is fate!" he said. "It is so you and I can talk."

Does it seem strange that I felt safe talking to this stranger? We were surrounded by other people and I expected Charles to rescue me at any minute. We passed the time talking!

"You must send me an invitation to your wedding. I will come," he declared and gave me his business card. Recently I learned from the Internet that he was who he said he was!

While we talked, I tried to devise a course of action. I had called Charles' apartment and received no answer. I did not want to call Charles' mother and alarm her. Lorrell sometimes stayed at Charles' apartment, but lived in a neighboring town. I did not have her phone number.

The night wore on, the hour grew late, and I decided to move to another part of the terminal. My new friend followed me. Actually, I felt his company was a security of sorts. He settled himself in the seat beside me, took my left hand in both of his and fell asleep. Was I taking care of him or was he taking care of me?

It was now past midnight. While he slept, I thought of what I might do. Could something have happened to Charles? Had he forgotten he was to pick me up? It had rained torrents. Might Charles have had a wreck on the way to the airport? A heart attack? I prayed to stay calm, to trust God. I waited.

Dawn arrived. My new friend left and I decided to call Charles at his apartment again. He picked up on the third ring. "Charles, what happened to you?" I asked.

"Where are you?"

"I'm at the airport. Did you forget me? I've waited all night long!"

"I was there!" he exclaimed. "Where were you? I didn't see you."

"I was sitting in the waiting room, waiting for you."

"I was late, ran through lots of water. I went into the airport and looked for you in the waiting area!" he said. "When I couldn't find you, I thought your flight had gone to Newark. I drove over there in the rain. There was water everywhere! By then, I was exhausted. I thought you changed your mind about coming. I came home and went to bed."

"What shall I do? I've spent the whole night holding hands with a stranger."

"You did what? You did what?" Charles exclaimed, twice.

"I'll tell you when I see you. What shall I do?"

"Stay where you are. I'm coming for you!" he said, and named a time.

When the time came and passed, I became anxious. I began to question his truthfulness. Finally, he arrived and explained that a flat tire on the way to the airport had detained him.

We stopped to visit his mother in Queens. After our greetings, she startled me by asking, "Why do you want to marry my son? You have three sons of your own."

I had no answer. I must have chuckled and shaken my head in puzzlement. Marriage and parental relationships are not comparable! By the time we left her, I no longer felt defensive, but our visit left me with many questions. Charles told me that his mother had opposed his marriage to Millie. Now I wondered why. Something Louise said indicated that she changed her mind about Millie before her death. What made Louise change her mind? Charles told me Millie managed the family finances. Maybe Louise gave her credit for that.

We left her apartment and found a diner. Again, I marveled at the goodness of the food. At the motel, I was neither indignant nor surprised that Charles expected me to go to bed with him. I did not intend to do that!

"You are trying to play me for a fool!" he accused.

"I don't play games! You and I are Christians. I'm sorry you don't understand, Charles. It's not right!"

Disgruntled, he soon left. If he didn't come back, how would I get back to New York City and the airport Sunday? Could I leave before? I spent a restless night even though I was more confident than I had been as a college freshman alone in a hotel room in Washington, North Carolina.

Next morning, he showed up again with his bags of bagels for his several family groups. For our breakfast, we ate bagels with cream cheese and began our journey. In Saratoga Springs, I checked into the motel where our engagement dinner was to be. Jean had invited us to have dinner with her family that evening. She had baked a birthday cake for me and she and her family made me feel very special.

The dinner party at the motel next evening included all of Charles' children, except Veronica. In addition, Charles had invited a young friend, also named Charles. Charlie came up to my room with us after the dinner party and he and Charles took turns playing a musical instrument that Charles had sold to him.

When the younger man spoke of his bewilderment since becoming a Christian about the rightness or wrongness of dancing and card playing, I said, "I do not believe playing cards or dancing makes one less a Christian."

Charles became agitated, accused me of belittling him before the younger man. Charles' anger ignited mine. I had an adrenaline surge. I grabbed one of the stuffed chairs and moved it across the room.

When his young friend left, I expected Charles to go too. However, Charles thought he was spending the night with me. I expected him to spend the night with Jean and her family. I reminded him that I had told him I wanted my own quarters. He left, but soon returned and insisted that I allow him to sleep there. It was very late and everyone had long since gone home. I felt trapped! He lay down, turned his back to me and fell into a deep sleep and I finally fell asleep.

Back home, I thought of giving him back his ring and calling off the marriage. He wrote, apologized for his behavior, and asked my forgiveness. Forgiveness was not an option. I had to forgive him. I did not have to marry him! There were many reasons to dissuade me: Charles' erratic behavior, his large family, Veronica's illness, our dissimilar upbringing. Eddie's protest: "How can you think of marrying a Northerner?"

While Eddie's reason was ridiculous – his father Don came from Massachusetts – it gave me pause. I think the reason I failed to break off at that juncture was because I believed we partnered with God and that our marriage would succeed against all odds.

CHAPTER

5

Planning a wedding was a new experience. Don and I married secretly February 1947 in Chapel Hill, intending to repeat the ceremony the following September at Hatteras. However, the turn of events that spring of 1947 canceled those plans. Don did not want to go to Glencoe, Illinois, where he would work that summer, without me. I canceled my plans for recovering credits I lost when I transferred from Woman's College of UNC my sophomore year. Instead of going to summer school, I would go with him. We called our parents and confessed our deception. Don asked Coach Kenfield, his employer, to help us, and he arranged for me to have a job at the Glencoe Country Club with the summer staff. He found a room for us through the housekeeper at the club. She had a neighbor, a widow, with an extra bedroom in an upstairs apartment who rented to us. Mrs. Massin was her name and she spoke several times of how tired we looked when we arrive after our long bus ride to Chicago from Chapel Hill.

I thought Charles expected to have guests and a celebration. We ordered wedding invitation – **We Love in the light of His love** – and my friends began to rally around.

Nancy Moore became anxious at my snail's pace and invited me to supper one evening so that she and her husband Randy could help me make a guest list and address the invitations. Nancy and Shirley Durham went with me to look for a dress. We went into a store and the first dress that I tried on, a street-length ecru lace with a wide collar and low, round neckline, fit me perfectly. It was both beautiful and affordable. I felt it had been waiting for me.

Choosing a matron of honor was difficult. There were three sisters and each dear in their own right. Margie, the oldest and a victim of multiple sclerosis was now confined to a wheel chair. I had been my youngest sister Mona's attendant the year before and she and I were close all our lives. I chose Jo, the sister five years older than I, because I wanted to honor her.

Nor was it easy to decide which of my three sons would walk me down the aisle, but I asked Eddie, the oldest. Charles' asked his oldest son Robert to be his best man, from four sons.

Before our wedding day, Andy told me that he and Debbie wanted to be married; and Cliff and Lynne decided they would marry. Lynne bought her wedding gown and I began to plan two rehearsal dinners in addition to my wedding. However, plans changed. Neither married that year. Cliff and Lynne severed their relationship some months later, and Andy and Debbie would marry later.

One day while Reverend Cameron, a former pastor of my home church, was visiting someone at Durham County Hospital, he and I had lunch together in the cafeteria. I asked him to honor his promise to dance at my wedding. His eyes widened, he slapped his forehead with his open hand, and he laughed. "Well, Sybil, you surprise me!" he said.

He agreed to translate The Lord's Prayer into movement for our ceremony and the choir would robe to sing special music of their choice as their gift to me. The congregation would sing "The Church's One Foundation."

Robert and Elizabeth Parker, members of my church, were to cater the reception and provide for 200 expected guests. Nancy Moore, who won blue ribbons at North Carolina State Fairs for her entries, volunteered to do my wedding cake. Elsie Webb volunteered to decorate the altar. Another church member, Virginia Spencer, a Durham florist, would do the flowers for the wedding party. The Reverend Hugh Cameron, a former pastor, and the present pastor, The Reverend Russell Stott, would coordinate our wedding service.

As the day for our wedding approached, Elsie Webb engaged her husband Arthur to come to my home with her to help me break with the past. Part of our strategy was to change my bedroom. Every morning when the sun touches the window of my present bedroom, I am happy for the change we made that day. I put away all my personal photos.

When the day arrived, my beautician friend Betty Allison did my hair. Another friend, Tillie Adams, did my makeup. I was as beautiful as their efforts could make me.

My sister Jo wore a street length gown of pink chiffon to accompany Eddie, in his tan suit, and me down the aisle. Robert Fetterroll stood with Charles, who looked handsome in his newly purchased dark blue suit. Chapel Hill friends and those from some distance came to share our joy and to fill Amity United Methodist Church.

The Reverend Stott's sermon at our Festival of Christian Marriage celebrated marriage and honored God. Lois Strother played the organ and Mary Comer's lovely soprano voice filled the sanctuary with the words of the Lord's Prayer. The Reverend Cameron honored my request, and wore the robe-like white stole, made for him by Dorothy Reynolds while he served Amity from 1971 to 1976. He stood in the middle of the chancel and made movements that heightened the meaning of the words Mary sang.

The choir sang John W. Peterson's "Shepherd of Love." The words "Forever I'll stay by your side ..." were poignant. Mary Comer and Betty Boling chose the duet they sang as Charles and I knelt at the altar.

United Methodism does not consider marriage a sacrament as the Catholic Church does. However, our intention was to have our ceremony glorify God and to proclaim Christ first in our lives.

After the reception, we drove south to Pinehurst for our first night together. The moon was growing to fullness and scientists attributed the blue moon some reported seeing in May 1983 to gases dispersed into the stratosphere by an erupted volcano in Mexico. However, we would enjoy a full moon on the ocean off Kiawah Island in South Carolina during our honeymoon, but we could not claim a true blue moon's luck for a true blue moon is when there is a second full moon in the same month.

We slept until late next morning. After a nice breakfast, we were on our way. As we approached Kiawah Island, the trees, mostly oak, were heavily draped with gray moss. We reached the entrance gate and a young, black female security guard requested reservation information, which we did not have. She wrote one for us and sent us on our way to find "Fiddler Three," the same cottage Mona and Bill rented for their honeymoon the year before, but we did not remember the number of the cottage. Luckily, I was able to retrieve the Kiawah folder with the information from my luggage and we were able to unload the car during daylight.

Settled in, we drank coffee, nibbled on food from our wedding food care package, ate bananas, and listened to the tape of our wedding ceremony, before we retired, too exhausted to make love.

Next morning, after a late and hardy breakfast, we walked on the beach, took pictures, and discovered treasures - coral encased in seaweed and other shells in the sand. Oleander was in bloom everywhere in the development.

When we returned to our cottage, we had glasses of milk, and looked at our forty-two beautiful cards of congratulations and listened to music. We made love and napped until 8 pm.

Glan Carlo Menotti, a Pulitzer Prize-winning Italian composer, Christopher Keene, and others founded Spoleto in 1977. They hoped to create an American counterpart to their annual Italian Festival of Two Worlds and chose historic Charleston, with its many theaters, churches and other performance spaces. For 17 days each spring world known artists entertain Charleston residents and visitors, so one day we drove to Charleston to attend Spoleto Festival USA.

We chose two of the performances at a host church. I knew the address, and drove the car along Charleston's narrow streets. Charles pointed the church out to me, but could see no available parking place. He became agitated, opened the door of the car, and jumped out into the street. Shocked, I had to keep going, circled the block, and came back to find him standing inside a picket fence watching the flow of automobiles. Exasperated, I stopped. "What would you have done if I had kept going?"

"I'd have got back somehow," he said.

"I don't think it would have been easy. Kiawah is not around the block."

After the performances, we took a harbor cruise to Fort Sumter, where in April 1861 Confederate troops bombarded the fort so heavily that it was surrendered to the Confederacy and the newly elected President Abraham Lincoln promptly used the event as a reason for raising a Northern Army to invade the South. That conflict between the North and South ended over 100 years before that 1983 Saturday afternoon, but the conflict between Charles (north) and Sybil (south) had just begun.

One morning, we were sitting by the swimming pool. Others were there too. Charles, grinning, said, "Let's talk about what we need to do about our sexual adjustment."

"Not now, Charles! Not here!" I whispered, hoping others by the pool had not heard him.

I could tell he was displeased when he stood up, paused briefly on the side of the pool, dove into the water, and swam away. Even to please him, whom I found attractive enough to marry, I was not comfortable discussing our sex lives with an audience!

On Sunday, we attended John's Island Presbyterian Church, founded in 1710, which we had seen on our way to Charleston. Since the complete renovation of their church was not done until 1992, I suppose the sanctuary we entered was the original building. There was a gate at the entrance of each pew to keep out drafts. I imagined the attendees of yore, plantation owners, their families, and their slaves, as we took our seats.

The Reverend Davies' sermon made me willing to let go of my resentment, against my new husband, which I had been wrestling with since the previous evening. With my intellect, I was ready to accept Jesus' words: "Forgive them, they know not what they do." I was ready to be reconciled. However, when Charles erupted in an emotional outburst when I commented about the sermon as we left the church, my anger was refueled as though he had added gas to my smoldering fire. Was every event to result in confrontation?

Without further incident, the week passed quickly and it was time to go home. We planned to go out to dinner for our last evening, but had a problem. We still had a large dish of leftover rutabaga that we had not eaten, because the large rutabaga had been enlarged even more by the addition of a potato, which Charles said his mother always added

Next morning, we said goodbye to our honeymoon cottage and started home. Somewhere in South Carolina, the 1980 Plymouth Horizon stopped running. We got out of the car, pushed it off the road to await assistance. The last day of our honeymoon trip was spent in a small South Carolina town waiting for a new water pump to be installed in the car.

CHAPTER 6

Charles left to return to his Nanuet apartment on June 4. Back in my own routine, I found our lack of affection during our two-week marriage disconcerting. We disagreed on so many things. Would we ever be able to live peacefully with one another? I had not been sad to see him go and wondered if I would ever want him to return. In a dream two nights later, I dreamed of kissing Don and I realized my new relationship lacked the tenderness and affection of my first marriage. Charles, more optimistic than I, had said, "We need to trust God."

Yes! I knew we needed time to adjust to one another, physically, emotionally and mentally. I did trust Charles for it was he who advised me to do a prenuptial agreement, which I had my lawyer prepare. It was he, who advised me to keep my name. "Why should you have to go through the trouble of changing your driver's license, deed to your home, and all the other?" he reasoned. I trusted God!

Money is said to be one of the biggest causes of friction in a marriage. We intended it not be one of ours. We would share the cost of utilities and food. Since the house was mine, I accepted taxes, insurance, and upkeep as my responsibility. We would have separate checking accounts. Money would not be our problem!

Back in New York, Charles went to visit his family in upper New York with his remaining vacation days. I expressed my misgivings in my journal: *Sometimes I think I married him because his little-boy-like enthusiasm makes me think of Don, that and his strong sense of family. But, he is not like Don in any other way. He nags and he is picky!*

His letter, dated June 8, reduced me to tears. He wrote of his desire to be the husband I needed. Time had enabled me to view the events of the honeymoon week with more objectivity, seeing there had been good times, as well as the disturbing. My anger had softened and I realized that I truly cared for him. We loved one another. Truly, I wanted to be the wife he needed.

We were not together for Father's Day, but Charles came on June 24, which was Andy's birthday. Andy, Cliff and Lynne came to have a nice dinner with us. After they left, Charles and I washed dishes together, talked in bed until the wee hours. Still later we had cake and milk. We looked deeply into one another's eyes and let our natural affection lead us to a deeper knowing of the other.

Charles flew back to New York on Sunday and went to Middle Grove the following weekend for a family celebration on Independence Day, which was on Monday. Jean called me at the hospital on Tuesday to tell me that he was in cardiac intensive care. "You don't need to come," she said. "He has his family here to take care of him."

"I am coming," I told her. *Wasn't I family?*

After her call, I worked until 3:30. Then I banked, bought airline tickets, and called Cliff before I went home to pack and dress. Cliff, a tennis professional at a private club in Durham, had rented a small house on University Drive in the east part of Durham. He and Lynne came for me and we arrived at the airport an hour before my 6:35 p.m. flight.

Jean, Lorrell and Willie met me at the Albany airport and took me to the Country Club Motel, which was near the hospital. After I checked in, we went to see Charles, who had been moved from the cardiac intensive care unit to a regular room two hours earlier. He had not had a heart attack, but had a touch of pleurisy. Oxygen tubes were still in his nostrils. "Sweetheart, you are really something!" he exclaimed.

I stooped to kiss him and teased, "You got sick so I'd come!"

The others left and I stayed with him until nearly midnight and slept late the next morning. After spending most of the afternoon with him, I walked back to the motel where Lorrell and Dubbie picked me up to take me to have dinner with Jean and the family. Charles would be discharged the next morning and after lunch with Jean, Lorrell drove Charles and me to Charles' apartment in Nanuet.

Next day, he and I walked to the mall to have his prescription filled, ate lunch at the Hungry Lion, and took a bus back to his apartment, since Lorrell still had his car. That night, he awoke me, out of breath. "I dreamed that I was dancing on my knees, trying to win your love," he said.

Lorrell still had his car the next day as well, so we walked to find a Chinese lunch and I bought my return airline tickets. We picked up some ice cream sandwiches to share with Lorrell and her husband, Lewis Wallace, who were to meet us back at Charles' apartment.

It seems that Charles had a lot of saved up vacation time that he was using before his retirement and I had some vacation time left as well. The following weekend found him again flying to

Raleigh-Durham for us to head for a Seven Devils rental cottage in the North Carolina mountains.

Our first morning, and every morning after, the sound of power tools in the hands of workmen near the cottage awakened us. After breakfast, we went onto the balcony, which overlooked a vast mountain range, to sit and talk. We spent most of our first morning sharing our histories.

During the week, we visited Tweetsie Railroad in Boone, N.C., located in a Wild West theme park in Appalachian Mountains. We took the three-mile ride on a historic steam railroad and enjoyed the live entertainment. That same evening, also in Boone, we attended Dr. Kermit Hunter's *Horn in the West*, an outdoor drama about the mountain peoples' struggle for freedom during the revolutionary war era. Daniel Boone was one of the characters.

We visited Grandfather Mountain, where the wind blew 45 miles per hour, and Mount Mitchell, the highest peak in the Appalachian Mountains range. Before 1845, when Texas was admitted to the United States, Mount Mitchell had the distinction of being the highest in the whole country.

When Saturday came, we thought we might finally enjoy a quiet mountain morning and sleep late. Instead, the sound of a lawnmower awakened us early.

"North Carolina is the best of the North in the South," a slogan aptly describes North Carolina. Charles had not yet seen it all. On our way east, we traveled along the Blue Ridge Parkway and stopped to enjoy the views. We spent a night in Chapel Hill at home and, the next day, drove to Hatteras, which is 500 miles from Seven Devils.

My sister Jo and her husband Carlos had just built a large addition to The Sea Gull Motel. They gave Charles and me the use of an efficiency apartment for the week and we invited Eddie to join us for dinner one evening. A few weeks earlier, he had met a young Canadian woman who was visiting Hatteras Island with her three-year-old daughter, her mother, and her mother's companion. He startled me by saying he planned to bring the young woman and daughter to Hatteras. I was dubious. Montreal, Canada, was farther north than New York, farther even than Massachusetts! What dare I say? I was reluctant to voice any objection, because I knew he would not listen. My oldest son was born sweet and willful, and comes from a long line of stubborn people. Well, perseverance against the hardships of life is a virtue!

After our visit to Hatteras, we came home to Chapel Hill. Charles returned to New York and I would fly to New York one more time, Thursday, August 11.

A terrific storm interrupted my flight into La Guardia and dumped much rain onto New York! Charles picked his way through back streets to avoid flooding to get to the airport. We were unable to see his mother that evening, which may have been fortunate. She was still angry that Charles married me.

Friday, after lunch, with Lorrell and her mother-in-law, Ruth Wallace, we went to see Veronica in the hospital. Veronica's social worker had persuaded her to commit herself, after they discovered her plan to travel to Williamsburg. Her doctor, reluctant to release her, relented, when Charles assumed responsibility for her and promised to bring her back promptly.

We took her to the bank to deposit the cashier's check she had written to cover the expense of her planned trip; then we went to her apartment. She liked another apartment better and put a deposit on it before we took her back to the hospital at 7:30 p.m. Words of an old song say, "I didn't ask, they didn't say, so I don't know," but I suppose Veronica, due to her schizophrenia, was a ward of New York State.

My life has been less frustrating since I learned to trust Christ to lead and protect me in my ignorance. Many things puzzle me about life and much has happened in mine that I do not understand. I never will in this life! Life's mysteries are in God's care. I must be content to leave them there.

That Saturday, we went to see the family upstate. We spent most of the time with Jean and her family. We even played a game of croquet. We returned to Nanuet before midnight and slept late the next morning. At noon, we left Nanuet and arrived at LaGuardia at one o'clock for my 2:10 p.m. flight.

Lynne came for Cliff to pick me up and took me to see his new apartment. My car was there. When I stopped by my church to pick up a bulletin from the morning service, the official board was meeting. So I stayed, landing squarely back into the middle of my busy life.

I called Charles, as he requested, when I got home. He was irritated and criticized me for asking about earlier rifts with his mother. I was stunned. I wrote in my journal that night, *Lord, don't let his anger touch me. Give me an understanding heart to love him and compassion to judge his actions with love.* After talking to him the following evening, for over an hour, I felt better.

News from Eddie was that Diane, the woman from Canada, and Faye, her three-year-old daughter, were with him and that he was content. He had driven to Montreal, Canada, to bring them to the Outer Banks. He did not tell me that Diane began to express doubts before they arrived on Hatteras Island.

Charles called with news that Lorrell and Lew had a baby son, whom they named Gavin, born August 16. Excited and pleased, he called his mother to tell her and hoped the news would make her forget her displeasure. He expected to obtain Veronica's release from the hospital the next day and to take her to see the new baby.

Andy, employed at a golf club, came home disgruntled one evening because he had been transferred from bartending to helping in the kitchen, which meant he got no tips. I longed to calm his spirit. My aunt's words came to my mind: "When they are little they ache your arms; when they are older they ache your heart."

I could not take them into my arms to rock them. To watch my sons struggle and suffer to learn truths they needed for their future happiness and success was painful. Their conflicts threatened my peace. I could not fix what needed fixing in their lives. Nevertheless, I forgot what I knew and I tried to comfort Andy.

CHAPTER

7

Charles would not come to Chapel Hill until September 19. I drove to Virginia Beach to be part of the wedding festivities surrounding the marriage of my great-niece, Bonnie Beck (Beth's daughter and my sister Marjorie's granddaughter). Bonnie married Jim Anderson September 10, 1983. I enjoyed sharing their happiness and being with family.

As I awaited Charles' arrival, I entertained guilt and self-doubts. Would the boundaries of my life be restricted with Charles in my life? He was only 62 years old going into retirement. I had offered to move to New York because I wondered what he would do with himself when he came to Chapel Hill. I admit I was relieved when he assured me that he looked forward to living in North Carolina. I did not want to leave my home, my friends, or my family. As he prepared to move, we discussed doing some kind of ministry, but not what it might be.

I was not there when Grant Hardware gave Charles the usual party prior to his last day of work, September 15. Four days later, he began his journey to Chapel Hill, pulling a U-Haul behind his car. Not yet out of New Jersey, a big tractor-trailer sucked his U-Haul under it, and turned his car completely around. The accident totaled his car. The contents of the U-Haul spilled over the roadway. Thank God, Charles walked away from the wreck, unscathed and determined. He rented a truck, loaded his possessions, with help I suppose, into the truck, and resumed his journey. When he arrived, I bounded down the steps, met him midway of the yard, and threw myself into his arms.

Charles left his family and all that was familiar to him to come to me. Now, recovering from the accident's trauma, he was without a car and thrown into idleness in a strange environment. His anger and depression seemed natural. My efforts to cheer him up and reassure him failed.

One afternoon when I arrived from work, the outside door stood open. "Hi honey, why is the door open? Someone might steal you," I said in jest and affection.

He bridled. I apologized. He said, "The day is over. Do not kid!"

At supper, he started to pour my coffee and I said, "Decaffeinated, please!"

He left the kitchen and I followed him to his bedroom. "You find fault with everything I do," he said. "I act like people treat me."

"Charles, I am not finding fault with you. I am sorry you think that I am."

At his suggestion, we registered to attend a series of Institute in Basic Youth Conflicts seminars in Greensboro in late October and early November. They covered ten areas: self-image, family, conscience, rights, freedom, success, purpose, friends, dating and commitment. His psychiatric wife Pat and he attended this program in New York. I suspect she initiated it after she recognized Charles' conflicts.

I thought I had confronted and resolved most of my youth conflicts. Seeking to understand life, I had read books by psychologists and psychiatrists, attended lectures, and studied Scripture, in addition to the help of my sessions with Dr. Somers. I had an open mind; I was willing to learn more, to embrace new truths for greater peace and spiritual freedom. I wanted our relationship to be all that it could be. Charles' response to physical intimacy puzzled me. When I asked him to wash my back, he said, "You have a right to your privacy."

I snuggled up to put my arm around him, and he rebuffed me: "Bedtime is for sleeping!" Even puppies and kittens snuggle.

In late October, after an exhausting day at the hospital, I came home to a sour-faced husband, who accused me of abusing and nagging him. All I had done was try to tell him that I stopped by our bank to update our accounts on my way home, because I thought he would be pleased with our gains.

My slow southern tongue was no match for his northern rhetoric. The words he flung hurt as though they were physical blows. After his outburst, we went for a walk around the block, but when we came home, he refused to eat supper and fell asleep in his easy chair while I read. When I was ready for bed, I covered him up and left him to sleep. I knew better than to try to breach his self-imposed exile. He slept on the couch and the next morning, as I was leaving for work, I said, "Goodbye, Charles. I hope you have a nice day."

"Nobody steps on me!"

"Not unless you put yourself under their feet. Have fun being mad," I said, as I opened the living room outside door.

"I usually do!"

"Yes, I've noticed that," I said and shut the door.

He was still sulking when I came home that afternoon and my repressed anger fired my energies. I took to the yard, trimmed the rose bush, lopped the hedges, cut one of the flowering quince to the ground, and I would have done the other if the light had lasted. I dragged the trash to the street, enjoying my own company and accomplishing the work I had suggested he might do to get outside in the sunshine and fresh air to gain relief from inactivity.

I had no warm feelings for Sir Charles. Let him work out his own problems. I would take care of mine! Perhaps it was one of Shakespeare's characters, maybe Othello, who declared, "Hell hath no fury like a woman scorned." I was furious!

Journal entry that night: *Lord, there are challenges to this relationship. I must love Charles or I'd call the police and ship him back to New York by air express. He is of no use to me sulking in the bedroom on Saturday night. I might as well be alone.*

Comfort him, Lord. Show him what he needs to know to be free of these destructive attitudes. Use this time to speak to the depths of Charles' soul. Give him the wisdom and courage to deal with the faults.

God, can You use two selfish clods of clay to express Your love in this old world, when we don't even know how to love one another?

The holidays went well. Andy and Debbie and Cliff and Lynne were in and out of the house for Christmas and came for New Year's dinner. Church activities, with the church family and others, were lovely and may have helped Charles feel less isolated and lonely. I enjoyed his happiness.

Don and I moved into our first home in Greensboro in 1951. After he left to teach in a junior high school across town, I was isolated and lonely without family or friends close by for support. I grew up in the middle of a small community, across the road from the schoolhouse and church, with Mr. Dolph Burrus' store on one corner across from us and Mr. Loran Ballance's "filling station" (gas) and pool hall on another corner. To the left of Burrus' store and Ballance's shop and, around the left corner, stood the U.S. Post Office, where Miss Maude O'Neal, our able postmaster (postmistress offended her sensibilities) reigned. Next to Mr. Dolph's store on the right, a road next to the U.S. Weather Bureau, led to Uncle Fred's home, fish house, and docks. We lived in the center of everything. People were in and out of my father's store and our living quarters all the time, providing a steady flow of social contacts. I was not prepared for the aloneness of our little community as I cared for three-year-old-Eddie and awaiting the birth of Andy.

Recently, I talked to Charles' sister Mildred by phone and she told me that their parents had owned an ice cream parlor and candy store in New York before the Great Depression. It figures that Charles missed the social contacts to which he had been accustomed as a child, and as a father of seven children.

Life had changed for both of us. I wanted him to enjoy his home with me, even while I bewailed my loss of creativity, my irregular journal entries. I missed the freedom to come and go without answering to anyone. His unhappiness was an affront.

For our first New Year's Eve meal, I included what was traditional - black-eyed peas for me, and lentils for him. We were part of the celebrations with others at church and with part of my family. The year 1983 ended on a happy note for us.

CHAPTER

8

Charles and I began the beautiful first day of 1984 with a walk and conversation. Debbie and Andy joined us for lunch and stayed to visit until nearly 5 o'clock. Charles was happy and affectionate. Even working ten straight days at the hospital was not bad when I could come home to a loving friend. I felt hopeful and looked forward to a happy year.

National news made us wonder if Jesse Jackson, a 1984 candidate for the Democratic presidential nomination, would be our first black president. Navy Lt. Robert O. Goodman Jr. had been shot down over Lebanon while on a mission to bomb Syrian positions in that country and was imprisoned. Jackson's visit with Syrian President Assad to secure his release was a success. Jackson became a hero!

Eddie and I were at odds. He wanted to add beer and wine to the inventory of the health food store in my building at Hatteras. I was unwavering in my opposition. At work, a new computer system challenged the pharmacy staff, especially Ben Bullock and me. Ben and I had worked together for Durham Hospital Corporation since 1967 and had gone through many pharmacy changes. I reminded Ben of our past flexibility and preached to myself. The computer changed the pharmacy routine and all of our lives forever. Once I charged an inordinate number of Dulcolax suppositories when I tried to make a correction. Instead of reducing the number charged, I added more. Some patient would surely scream, "Fraud!"

Around the middle of the January, Charles complained of not feeling well, and became peevish and difficult. He remained remote for the rest of the month. I left him alone and hoped his sense of humor would reappear soon. I moved the little blonde ballerina figurine in the red dancing costume away from the little boy in a white cap and blue knickers, but Charles never noticed, or acknowledged it if he did. I found diversion with my job and with church related activities, but our disharmony drained my energies.

When April came, Charles and I went on vacation, first to Upper New York to visit his family. His daughter Jean fed us several time and I enjoyed her family. We saw little of his four sons. They had their work. Most of the time, Charles left me alone in a motel room in Sarasota Springs while he sought the company of his offspring until I complained, "This is my vacation as well as yours!"

When we went back to New York, before our return south, we took the New York City Harbor and the Hudson River tours on a sailing vessel. Afterward, we drove to Virginia Beach to visit my niece Beth for a couple of nights. My cousin Minerva and her husband, Bill Johnson, invited us to lunch at their home in Norfolk before we left to visit our Hatteras family.

Lee and I still kept in touch and a letter from Kansas City told me that he had undergone cataract surgery March 22. He had been in the hospital in April with a serious separation of the retina.

Another surprise event in our family was the marriage of Andy and Debbie. Five days before our May 21 anniversary, they went to Hillsborough, Orange County's seat of government, during their lunch break. They were married by a justice of the peace. Perhaps they will decide to write their memoir and tell about that. Two sons and a daughter, in the middle, will be prominent characters in their narrative.

Another significant happening for me in May was the death of a family friend, Maurice Bernard Folb, fondly referred to as Doc Folb by Hatteras Island residents. He was a young U.S. Naval pharmacist mate serving on Hatteras Island and, in the absence of a doctor, in the '20s, when he attended my mother at my birth. Weighing in at ten pounds, I was named Sybil Bernadine, for him and the woman he was to marry, Sybil Miller of Buxton. Many grateful mothers named their children, using part of his name. There were: Louise Folb Oden, Maurice Stowe and Maurice Peele, O.B. (Oden Bernard) Peele, and probably others. He responded to help all he could in serious illnesses, like diphtheria, as well as broken limbs, or any medical emergency. Then, back at his quarters, he was required to write it up in the station log as first aid administered.

Of course, there were no cars and only sand rut roads on Hatteras Island in 1926. Mama and Daddy made a room available for Doc Folb's use whenever a venture kept him from returning to the U.S. Wireless Station in Buxton, ten miles north of Hatteras Village.

After Doc Folb's tenure as medical officer, the State of North Carolina offered to grant him a license to practice medicine, which he declined. He followed a career in public health, related to medicine, in Winston-Salem. My family and I visited him there several times while we lived in Greensboro. Once he told me that during my birth my mother prayed the most beautiful prayer that he ever heard. I believe God touched me then and has always held me close to His heart.

After retirement, Doc Folb retired to a home he built in Buxton and to the people whom he loved, and who loved him. Charles and I visited him at his home in Buxton shortly before his death.

A new, startling chapter in our story opened on our trip to Hatteras in 1984. Before his death in 1962, my father traveled to every courthouse that might hold information to identify the heirs to the property that once belonged to his great-grandmother, Courtney Ballance, wife of the first William Dudley Austin. After untold hours of research to identify and find the heirs to the property, he purchased the small plots and obtained deeds to make up the 13 acres of land that he willed to his heirs. The property was in litigation when he died in 1962, but when it went to court after his death, the courts decided in favor of his estate. My Brother Shank, administrator of his will, made the division of the property among the six heirs - my siblings, the lawyer, and me - in 1975. Shank had died in 1976. I never expected the controversy that now plagued us.

Mona and Bill's cottage was already under construction on her lot, and Charles and I were staking out the site for our cottage when we received notice of a lawsuit brought against my siblings and us, by Howard Phipps and wife of New York State. Attorney Wallace H. McCown, whom our father had hired on contingency to defend his and our rights to the 13 acres of land, was the sixth heir sued.

In late September, the specter of the Phipps legal matter had my full attention. We needed a delay. I made an appointment with my lawyer, hoping he might advise me. I engaged him, but after the first month, I knew I would be unable to afford the cost of individual counsel and was relieved when we heirs learned that we could act as a body. We decided to hire a Dare County lawyer and were fortunate to be referred to Roy Archbell, an attorney in Southern Shores with a reputation for land disputes such as ours.

There was cause for my fear and discouragement. I felt so overwhelmed that I questioned if the land were worth the worry. However, in mid-October, Mona, Bill, Charles and I went to Hatteras to consult with others in the case.

My proximity to the University of North Carolina Library and the North Carolina Archives in Raleigh made it plausible for me to do some of the research. It would be less costly for everyone and I would be compensated by the group for my work. Research took us back to 1711-1712. At the North Carolina Archives on Jones Street in Raleigh, I perused old files and tapes in search of marriage banns, deeds, and land transfers. I looked for any evidence that might strengthen our claim and learned more and more about the formation of the families, particularly the Austin family, from the tax rolls and censuses of Hatteras Banks.

Before 1846, Hatteras and Ocracoke villages were on the same island and in the same county. A storm that year opened Hatteras Inlet and separated them. Fifty miles or so north, the same storm cut Oregon Inlet, to separate Bodie Island from Pea Island. As our search progressed, we became familiar with much of the topography of Hatteras village and surrounding ground.

Hatteras Banks had been in Currituck and Hyde counties during different periods of its history. For all we know, Hatteras Banks may have been under the jurisdiction of Craven County in 1712; or of Carteret County, formed from a part of Craven County in 1722; or even a part of extinct Bath County. When Charles and I visited our Atlantic Beach timeshare, I visited Carteret Courthouse and went through very old deed books and records there, but found nothing of interest to our cause.

In 1870, Dare County was formed from land formerly in Currituck, Hyde, and a small part that had once been part of Tyrrell

County. During our research, we visited the several county seats and their courthouses, as my father had. Records at the Currituck Courthouse might have been helpful to many seeking information. However, a fire in the 1800s destroyed the earlier records and the courthouse.

Charles accompanied me as we visited Hatteras Island graveyards. He made sketches of some tombstones that he found fascinating, while I searched for names and dates among the dead of any former heirs of the land.

The identity of Suzanne Stow - later this family name became Stowe- still haunts me. In 1790, she sold a large tract of land to W.B. Ballance, the father of Courtney Ballance, who married William Dudley Austin, my father's great grandfather. Courtney had received a share of the land when her father died.

We examined military records searching for Suzanne, suspecting she may have been a Revolutionary War widow. I dreamed of finding her grave in the old graveyard at Beaufort, which Charles and I visited while we vacationed at Atlantic Beach. While we looked, someone told us a story about a man who died at sea and had been pickled in a barrel of rum. When the ship reached land, he was buried, barrel and all, in the Beaufort cemetery. We never found Suzanne's identity; who her husband might have been; or where she settled after selling her Hatteras property to W. B. Ballance.

Attorney Archbell learned that Georgia Gaskins, a village woman I knew as a child, attempted in the early 1900s to acquire the land we were defending by a land grant. Our claim was the same as one of the two tracts she sought to acquire. This had to be fully explored to its conclusion.

A late journal entry: *I feel like I'm living 200 years ago as I research ... My findings indicate that the Eastern part of North Carolina adhered to land laws and engaged in more tourism in early times than I ever imagined. Newspapers posted the arrivals of guests to the Nags Head summer resort each week. Interestingly, room and board cost two dollars a day, or twelve dollars a week. A few years later, the price dropped to ten dollars a week.*

Attorney Archbell requested I look for the John W. Rollinson diary in the Carolina Collection of UNC Library. I found it and read his short, fascinating account of the era of a porpoise factory on Hatteras Island. Both my grandfather and my father had been employed there at some time during its 100-year activity, but I saw nothing that related to the case at hand.

Since my only experience with research had been for a freshman English research paper, I thought my efforts slower than another's would have been. To garner tidbits of information sometimes took hours. However, I found unexpected, unrelated information concerning people of my childhood: a suit over fishing nets; a divorce and a child custody case; the handwritten will of George Charles Daniels of Wanchese, my mother's father. Memories came alive! I imagined the lives of the generations before and wished they had been kind enough to arrange the similar names in different generations in chronological order so I knew which one belonged where.

Our lawyer accumulated over 1000 documents before the end of the litigation. These documents are now part of the Dare County Historical Archives and available for use by the public.

With our cottage venture thwarted, Charles and I considered erecting a cottage on the property next to the building Eddie and his family occupied. Charles would love living across the highway from the post office. However, Eddie wanted to own that property intact. He discouraged me from building there. I decided to spruce up what we had, and Charles and I stopped in Carrboro one morning to talk to a kitchen cabinet vendor. We committed and then visited a store having a carpet sale. When the time came, Charles removed the old cabinets and supervised installation of the new ones and the carpet.

We had a garden, and we sometimes worked there together. Sometimes Charles volunteered to cook while I worked in the garden. We attended church regularly and he participated with the church group that I facilitated in my home each week. However, one night after they left he accused me of being a "know it all." He could not let it go, but kept on nagging and nagging. Seemingly, my leadership role was a threat to him.

That weekend we attended a writing seminar at the Aqueduct Christian Conference Center in Chapel Hill. Presenters were David Hazzard and Leonard LeSourd. Friday evening when we checked in, I thought the heaviness and pain, which radiated down the right side of my face and over my right eye, might be due to a sinus infection. While others raved about the seminar, I remained lethargic and in pain. On Saturday evening, I claimed the healing prayers the Reverend Tommy Tyson offered.

Sunday, our last day, I prayed: *Dear Father, I know you are with me and want to heal me; to provide freedom from this pain. My discouragement is the opposite of trust. Please forgive my lack of faith and help me with this battle, which is yours.*

When I went to work on Monday, my right eye was red and there were two blisters on my right forehead at the hairline. The doctor in the hospital infirmary said, "It is not pink eye."

He sent me to McPherson Eye Ear Nose Throat Hospital, where a physician identified it as herpes zoster, or shingles. "Would you be interested in being part of a study in progress at Duke Hospital?"

he asked, explaining that prednisone was the only alternative he could offer.

He left me alone to decide. I sat in the examining chair in that sterile, white sanctuary, and I prayed. Why should I fear what God provided? I decided to accept the chance to be a part of the Burroughs-Welcome acyclovir study.

During my confinement, Charles took good care of me, leading me about when I could not see; taking me to and from the appointments with the Duke ophthalmologist. Once he brought me a dripping pistachio ice cream cone and I sat in bed laughing while the sodden treat slid down my hand. Another amusing incident of that time was a telephone call from a woman promoting Atlantic Beach property. I was lying on the living room couch. I responded: "I can't go to Atlantic Beach to look at property. I'm involved with a case of shingles."

She closed the conversation, "Good luck with your house."

First startled, I began to laugh. "Oh, Charles, she thinks I am shingling a roof!"

Thankfully, I received the medication instead of the placebo. My illness was shortened by the acyclovir I received. I was able to go back to work on June 26 and we were able to attend the fifth Austin Family Reunion, at Hatteras, July 1, 1984.

The first U. S. Census listed three Austin brothers and their father Thomas Austin as heads of families. Daniel, a fourth brother was unmarried. Thomas Jr., Cornelius, and William sired children to help populate early Hatteras Village. Approximately 200 of the 318 living members of our branch of the tree, descendants of my grandparents William Wheeler Austin and wife Mogieannah Oden Austin, were present to celebrate our long, proud heritage. Mona and Bill came from Clemmons to occupy their new cottage for the first time.

In early August, I was miserable and sleepless due to indecision. Eddie was pressuring me to sell him the property in the village and I was hurt that he had sold many of my mother's possessions, my possessions, in a yard sale. I did not want to sell the house to him. Yet I was not sure I wanted to take back the responsibility of the property by evicting him either. Buster Farrow was waiting for me to have the beach land surveyed so he could begin to build a house for Charles and me. I did not know whether to see a lawyer, a psychiatrist - maybe both!

When we received another invitation to go to Atlantic Beach to look at property, we went and ended up buying a timeshare, since I had decided to sell Donald Edmund Skakle Jr. the property left to me in 1969 by my mother. However, Eddie had agreed that I could retain the smallest of the four apartments. Then Charles and I could visit Hatteras without inconveniencing anyone. With that in mind, Charles and I set up the apartment with dishes, coffee pot, flatware, and linens and were very pleased with it and used it a couple of times.

Debbie and Andy were building a house in Cary, North Carolina. Debbie worked as a pharmacist intern for Eckerd's and Andy worked as a maintenance man at the apartment complex, where they lived while he pursued a master's degree in physical education administration at Carolina.

Charles' and my home projects were still in progress. Only I knew that the bookshelves, which Charles moved to the space between the chimney and the outside wall of our dining area, were supposed to be there. They fit perfectly. It was my fault they were placed as they were, on the outside of the utility closet nearer the kitchen, to accommodate the telephone.

Until mid-September, I attempted to cook without a stove and the carpet installation came still later.

My sister Margie's husband, Curtis Newton, went into the hospital in Greensboro the middle of September. Charles and I stopped to see him and spent Friday night with Margie, on our way to the mountains. We stopped back by the hospital on our way home on Monday and he was in isolation. On Wednesday, we learned that Clifford Curtis Newton Jr. had died that morning at four o'clock, October 8, 1984.

Journal - *Charles calls himself sanguine, meaning he is confident, upbeat, optimistic, cheerful! Sometimes he lives up to this description. I consider myself optimistic, so what's the problem? Now he is in another slump, irritable and hard to please. And instead of feeling sadness and compassion for him, I am selfish and want him to be available when I need him. I have always been this way, or Charles and I are ill matched.*

Our pastor, Russell Stott, came for a visit. Charles opened up and talked to him of his anger and pain, while I felt shut out and ignored. Stott's suggestion that I call someone and get involved seemed like a criticism of me. I was involved!

Charles went to bed without saying goodnight and I called Lee, at 12:30 at night! Kansas City time is an hour earlier. It felt good to talk to Cowpoke. I do not think that our pastor had in mind for me to call Lee. But I needed to talk to someone too!

Debbie and Andy, Debbie's parents and her sister Susan, and Cliff joined us for Thanksgiving dinner. Thanksgiving propelled us into Christmas activity, and as the holidays approached, I became, as I had for years before, full of sadness and dread rather than joy.

I needed Charles' goodwill. December 22 journal entry reflects my mood.

Christmas disappoints me. Christ never does. All the glitter makes it hard to keep my eyes on Him, to be what He wants me to be. God, be enough!

The pharmacy holiday shift fell to me that year, and I worked all day on Christmas Eve. Work was lighter than usual. Cliff joined us for the evening church service and after work on Christmas Day, Debbie, Andy and Cliff joined us for spaghetti, a unique Christmas meal. With our energies saved, we enjoyed opening our gifts and being together all the more.

The night after Christmas, Charles had reservations for us at Slug's to celebrate the holiday and our first dinner date. We came home, listened to tapes, and danced to one of them. Since he had danced at Roseland in New York as a youth, he felt qualified to instruct me. I never had a lesson; I only danced to a jukebox at The Beacon in Hatteras as a girl. His prompts kept me from hearing the words of the song and feeling the rhythm of the music. It would have been sweet if he had simply held me and we had danced, enjoying the romance of the moment, but I did not dare tell him how I felt.

Exhausted by the doings of Christmas and nine straight days of work at the hospital, I slept until two o'clock the next day and so did Charles.

CHAPTER 9

Stephanie Snow was born January 10, 1985 in Canada on a snowy day, which happened to be my birthday too. Diane's Canadian citizenship entitled her to free health care, so Eddie, the struggling commercial fisherman, took her to Canada for the birth of the baby. Eddie told me they married the summer before. This new baby was the first that had both Don and my blood and I was delighted. I had not been happy about the twins Diane miscarried the year before. They were boy and girl twins and lived only a few hours.

The search for clues continued in the litigation case. In early March, I found an important document that Attorney Archbell wanted. A staff member of the NC Archives in Raleigh copied it for me. (Today an attorney could find that record by Internet without leaving his office, probably.) As we suspected, the document proved that erosion had eaten away the shoreline of much of the land we were defending; and since the first taxes were paid for it in 1755. However, the document did not help our case at all.

May 30, 1985, I signed the bill of sale for Eddie to own the property inherited from my mother. In May too, a devotion I wrote, which paralleled the distress of a little girl in my care and my feeling of abandonment at Don's death, was accepted by *The Upper Room*, a publication of the United Methodist Church, and appeared in the May issue. These were important events for me. A disappointment was that Eddie needed the money and rented "my" apartment. When I complained, he said, "You can stay with us!"

Before Charles and I married, we had talked of ministry and a simpler, quieter life. By retiring, I hoped to improve my relationship with Charles and to prevent regret. I turned in my letter of intent at Durham County Hospital June 12, 1985. I worked my last day June 29. At age fifty-nine, I was three years short of eligibility for partial Social Security benefits from Don's account. Gratefully, I learned that as beneficiary of Don's teacher pension, I was eligible for coverage under the North Carolina Teacher's Retirees Insurance Plan with Blue Cross-Blue Shield for health insurance. Fortunately, we learned that by paying his part of the premium, Charles might receive coverage too.

Perhaps my talk of retirement was what prompted Eddie to voice his hurt concerning his father's failure to leave a will that mentioned him. Actually, he was the only one provided for by Don's North Carolina Teacher's Retirement account, opened in 1950 when Eddie was two years old. Don had failed to update his beneficiary designations to include Andy and Cliff. In order for me to receive Don's pension, Eddie signed off as beneficiary when Don died. I feel sure they all knew their father did not intend it to have been that way. He did not expect to die so early. All we had was a handwritten will, written when he and I were ready to take a trip to Maine in 1974 to celebrate his father's 80th birthday. Poppa Skakle and his wife Beth, who lived in Florida during the winter and went to Cape Cod for their summers, were guests of Don's older brother Gordon and his family that August. Luckily, we found Don's handwritten emergency will among his clothing in a bureau drawer in 1980. According to that will, all would go to me, if I survived him. Otherwise, he requested his three sons share equally.

Sibling rivalry is the theme of novels, the cause of court cases, and underlying emotional conflicts of the clients of psychiatrists, and psychologists! Bible stories of Cain and Abel, Esau and Jacob, and Joseph and his brothers tell troubling stories of jealousy, as does the story Jesus told about a prodigal son and his older brother. The older brother's attitude toward his errant brother grieved the father.

In a letter sent to each of them, I attempted to reassure them of their father's love and mine. If anything remains of my estate when I am gone, I trust they will honor me by remembering and acting with cooperation and affection for one another as they carry out my wishes and execute my will. Each is loved equally well, if not the same, for each one is different. Their response to me and mine to each of them is individual.

Just before my retirement, the Reverend Richard Holbrook entered our lives. He requested financial help, which we could not give, for his ministry. However, Charles volunteered to teach a bunch of 11 to 14-year- olds from 9 to 3 on weekdays in July. My feelings about Holbrook and his ministry were ambivalent and I resented that Charles volunteered when I was retiring to be with him. Besides, I was grieving. I knew grief would be a natural consequence of leaving my profession. Charles did attempt to cheer me up, to make me laugh.

A journal entry the latter part of June concerned an entirely different subject: Terrorism! *Can we deal with the terrorism that is tearing at our peace? Can President Reagan turn the tide? Those responsible for hijacking TWA Flight 847 held 39 American passengers prisoners 17 days*

*and murdered a United States Navy diver, Robert Stethem, in their demand
for the release of 735 Lebanese Shiites held by Israel.*

Terrorism did not abate during President Ronald Reagan's term
of office nor since. (The destruction of the Twin Towers in New York
City on September 11, 2001, shocked our country, and others, into
greater vigilance against the elusive enemy. We wage a war on all
fronts in an effort to eliminate this terrible threat to life and the
security of the world.)

One afternoon when I went to bring Charles home, he was
limping from having wrenched his back taking chairs out of a car
while working with the ministry. His anger seemed aimed at me.
Sometimes people lash out at those who care about them, but his
criticism and abuse aroused my ire, feeding my feelings of neglect.

Nevertheless, we prepared to attend the Prayer and Bible
Conference at Lake Junaluska, a United Methodist Conference
Center in Western North Carolina. I hoped the magic of that place
would work a miracle and that he would enjoy it too.

We stayed overnight with Mona and Bill in Clemmons and
continued west the next day. I loved the beautiful environment and
comfortable accommodations among loving brothers and sisters
in Christ. He was interested in the programs and studies, some
different from mine. I especially enjoyed one with Robert Dungy:
"Dream Interpretation." Dungy said, "Awake, or asleep, God invites
us to wholeness."

"Our dreams are necessary to balance our emotions, spirit and
soul. While there are universal symbols, each of us has individual
symbols. Seek to pay attention to and to understand their meaning
for you," he advised.

Charles related a dream, which I shared with him, to a couple
from Oklahoma with whom we ate. The dream was about him

and Don showing up to prevent my meeting the man to whom I was engaged when I was seventeen. I did not mind, for they were members of the dreams class with me. As I write this, I believe my dream warned me. My former fiancé came back into my life ten years after this dream, declared his love, and then walked away again, without explanation.

Remember Joseph's story in the Bible? "Pay attention to your dreams."

My memoir, *Valley of the Shadow*, tells about a tour, which Dr. Maxie Dunham led to attend Oberammergau Passion Play in 1980, of which I took part. He was the featured speaker of the conference and one of the reasons I wanted to attend.

A new journal entry - *I want to blame Charles for my discontent. Ultimately, I am responsible for my own happiness. Perhaps, if I were more generous, less selfish, my concern for his welfare would overcome my restraint. Charles has a problem with impotence. Perhaps he is afraid of failure. I dread rejection and do not even want to help. That and his lack of affection, and that he might fail again keep me immobilized. How can prostitutes do what they do? I need foreplay, while he thinks he should not make me an object of his desire. But I am his wife!*

We had a busy two weeks in August when Charles' grandchildren, Dubbie (Jean Marie) and Paul, came to visit. We visited Guilford Battleground; went on a picnic at Jordan Lake. We drove to Raleigh to have them see he Museum of Art and the Capitol Building, as well as other historical sites. We even took them out to play tennis. Torn between pleasure at their visit and my selfishness, I wrote in my journal, *God, I'm glad you love me because I dislike me very much. I think of the patience and generosity of my mother, and Don's mother, with new gratitude. I hate the irritability, anger, selfishness I find in my heart. Surely, I was not like this with my children. I'm ashamed, God, please forgive me.*

Charles found such pleasure with them. I was busy with the tasks of taking care of things. He played games with them while I cooked dinner. At the beginning, I asked they not turn on the television except for the time agreed and confronted them when they did. Then I beat myself up for taking up for my rights. I felt like Satan had me on a yo-yo string. I wanted to feel loving, but could not get back to a safe place in my emotions.

The morning they were to fly back to Albany, New York, Paul cried. He did not want to go home. I loved them, but their visit showed me again my great need of God's grace and mercy.

"Selfishness is not living as one wishes to live, it is asking others to live as one wishes to live." Ruth Rendell.

I am selfish. Yet, I am no less virtuous than others. We fight on different battlefields, but selfishness is universal. It is the cause of wars! If we could, we might all be despotic. A two-year-old is a little tyrant who thinks his way is the way it must be. Despotism would not bring me happiness. To be happy is to love. To love is to respect others' rights. I have a right to have my rights respected, as well. Different expectations cause conflict, but need not cause division. Love and respect work together to find solutions!

Robert, Charles' oldest son, wrote that he and Susan would now have a wedding. They had a baby son about a year old. I was glad that Charles would not insist on driving to Sarasota Springs to participate. I wrote in my journal, *I love the crazy guy. He is funny when he is not utterly ridiculous, or using his humor to manipulate an advantage.*

Marriage is many things. It is a business. It can be an intimate, fleshly, spiritual oneness. It can be a sharing of the daily life with another with loyalty, integrity, honesty, and compassion. It requires sympathy, made wise by empathy, to be all it can be.

Hundreds of tiny threads strain and stretch to hold a marriage together. The more rigid threads keep the elastic ones from too much expansion and distortion. When the contrasting threads move against one another, the warmth, hope, romance of the soft colorful threads in the pattern restore harmony.

Charles believed duty took over and that courtship ended after marriage. I disagreed. The game changes, but spouses should still enjoy playing by flirting, joking, jesting. My playmate did not want to play. He seemed to lack spontaneity and confessed that in order to engage in sexual activity he needed to program himself.

In the midst of this, Charles told me of his mother's concern about a will. Maybe it was his will. It may have had nothing to do with me. When Charles asked me to talk about wills, I was dumbfounded. Our prenuptial agreement relieved us of responsibility for the other. As far as I knew, he had his pension, Social Security, and owned nothing more. We married for love and companionship. He gave Julie his home in their divorce agreement. Sometime before we married, he gave his daughter Jean the 100 acres in Middle Grove, New York, which his children's mother had acquired. That is what he told me. Jean stepped up to care for her younger siblings after their mother died. His giving Jean his heritage may seem similar to my selling mine to Eddie. Motivation to rid himself of responsibility for the property may have been what it was for him too.

The Bible instructs women to respect their husbands, regardless of their strength of character. It teaches men that they should love their wives "as Christ loved the Church." One teacher theorized that women sometimes have trouble respecting their husbands. We know that all men do not cherish their wives. God knows what promotes harmony and growth in the marriage relationship, but we students get confused about the why in human experience. Lois Wyse seems to think there may be another problem affecting us: *"Men are taught to apologize for their weakness, women for their strength."*

I wanted to respect Charles, who I knew needed outlets for his immense energies. I contacted my friend Ed Brecht, who belonged to a bowling league. Ed introduced Charles to his group and thereafter, Charles enjoyed the weekly game and the people he met. I could not bowl due to a hand injury. Instead, I wrote and submitted articles and poems with some success. Editors are subjective and decide what to accept.

Sometime during 1985, Governor James G. Martin of North Carolina declared "The Year of the Child." Something must have prompted me to write him of my concern this late in the year. I do not remember what it might have been. My concern was/is real. "We need to give as much thought and effort to provide a safe moral environment for our children as has been given and is being given to discourage cigarette smoking."

The fight against tobacco, begun years before, intensified. Education and legislation waged war against tobacco while moral and spiritual threats against our children went unchallenged. Education against alcohol is needed, as well. Alcohol causes crime, addiction, misery, violence, suffering, poverty. Intensive education similar to that against tobacco might yet promote a less violent, saner, safer, sweeter society. Education and fear of cancer reduced use of tobacco in the United States. What will it take to deglamorize alcohol?

That October a dreadful tragedy took the lives of Elsie Webb's husband Art and their son Art (jr.), when their small private plane hit the top of the trees at Horace William's Airport as they attempted to land. The plane caught fire. Elsie's other friends and I felt helplessness, while Elsie herself, fortified with the first phase, denial, exhibited her usual prayer-warrior durability and courage in face of grief.

The day after Thanksgiving, the dog in our lives, Nikki, a 14-year-old, white spitz, needed to be put to sleep. We consulted Andy first. Nikki belonged to Monica Daniels, to whom Andy was married for eighteen months thirteen years earlier. Nikki came to live with us, and our dog Suki, when Andy and Monica moved into an apartment. When Monica was ready to move on, she asked if we would like her to take Nikki. Don said "No!"

When we took her to the vet's, Charles stood at Nikki's head, touching her to comfort and reassure her, as Dr. Vine gave the injection. We left her body with them for disposal.

God gave man dominion over the animals, but not over other human beings. A man in Florida, out of love and compassion, ended his wife's suffering and was convicted and imprisoned for manslaughter. Neither his daughter nor we condemned him. Like him, we believed love dictated our action when we had Nikki put to sleep. We were relieved that Nikki's suffering and ours was over. The uncertainty, the waiting, the fluctuation between hope and despair are hard to bear. I questioned my intent, as the Florida husband must have done. Was the decision made to finalize Nikki's suffering or mine? We grieved Nikki, a good dog - a true friend.

December arrived. We lighted the Chrismon tree at Amity UMC. Mine was one of the seventeen voices when the choir sang "Gloria" by Antonio Vivaldi, and I felt like Minnie Pearl doing opera. Our choir leader, Lois Strother, at the piano had two violins, a clarinet and oboe to accompany her.

Year ended. Debbie anticipated receiving her pharmacy license in January. Andy, still working on his master's degree in physical education administration, spoke of going for a doctorate. Cliff, living in Carrboro, considered going back to school to complete his requirements for teacher certification.

CHAPTER

{ 10 }

In early January 1986, I made only two journal entries. The first entry concerned my friend Mary Sigrist who, back home in Maryland, had learned that she had cancer. I telephoned, hoping that somehow my love for her would make a difference.

The second entry, three weeks later, consisted of a list of happenings, the most startling of which was a call from UNC Memorial Hospital on January 24, at 1:20 a.m. Cliff was in emergency and they needed my permission to perform surgery. The admitting doctor feared his carotid artery may have been severed in a car accident, an accident in which he hit a utility pole as he took a corner too fast. The surgeon did not wait. Before I was able to get to the hospital, he had found the artery intact and stitched up the long, angled gash on his neck. The hospital kept him overnight and he was discharged around lunchtime the next day. Our lives resumed their frantic pace as though nothing of consequence had happened.

A few days later, Cliff, who had been working as a bartender, flew to New York to take a position with *TV Update*. His career development had been stuck. It seemed more like floating than swimming. His employment with *TV UPDATE* gave him a chance to redirect his life and his energies and proved that he had an aptitude for salesmanship. As he went about the country selling advertising, he was soon wooed and hired by a natural gas company in Michigan. Tired of motel rooms, he decided to make Milwaukee, Wisconsin his home base.

Charles and I went to Hatteras in April, and I learned that Eddie's boat, in the shipyard for repairs in Frisco, was up for sale. Diane was unhappy and Eddie, wretched. I wanted to help, but was overcommitted because the land litigation continued to stretch my emotions and my finances. Lawyer bills had depleted my small savings.

Fishing is never predictable, but my optimistic oldest son believes his glass half-full rather than half-empty. He tried to reassure me that things would be better soon. He and Diane had plans to open the store, which he expected to solve his money problems. I wanted them to have the satisfaction of solving their own. When his father and I were students and first married in 1947, and after Eddie's birth in 1948, we depended on Don's G.I. benefits. For two years, we lived in a 6' x 12' trailer, bought for $600. The summer Eddie was due to be born, Don was with his college coach, John Kenfield, teaching tennis lessons in Glencoe, Illinois, to earn the money to pay for the hospital and doctor's bills. I wanted my sons to grow strong in the struggle, but it was painful to watch and not try to help.

Cliff returned home April 30 to answer the charge in court for the January 24 car accident. He was scared and so was I. We were very grateful when the arresting officer failed to show and Cliff did not have to face the charges. We knew God's mercy was undeserved.

Cliff returned to his employment, and Charles and I had a terrible fight one night in late May. The television show was violent and I requested that we watch something else. He flared, "You squeeze me under your thumb, while you do as you please."

He was so angry that he slept in the outdoor storage shed overnight. I checked on him at 3:30 a.m. Next morning, when I looked out the kitchen window, he was watering the garden in his pajamas, perhaps hoping that the neighbors would never know he slept outside all night.

The compensation I received for the paralegal work helped my financial situation a little, but not nearly enough. I needed more money. Eckerd's hired me to do pharmacy relief work in Durham, Chapel Hill, and Burlington. Their computer programs were different from those at Durham County Hospital. I did not understand their nightly backups. One night, alone and doing an evening shift, I panicked when one of the printers stopped working and I could not rectify the problem. I decided that night that I would resign as soon as I could fulfill the commitments already made.

When I tried to engage Charles, who was more remote and irritable, to discuss our differences, he replied, "No comment."

He said, later that same day, "I care more than you know."

We both cared, but we needed professional help. We could not wish or pray away our complex problems in our marriage. Ironically discord in Soweto, South Africa, during a World Cup Soccer competition made news that caught my attention. Thousands were there to support their nation's teams when brave young people, some as young as 12 years of age, took a stand against apartheid, and many died. Conflict at home and abroad!

Charles and I went to Hatteras for Independence Day to attend the Austin Reunion. We stayed in our little apartment in Eddie's building. We expected Lynne and Cliff, but they failed to show. The reunion, held on the lawn of Aunt Beatty (Beatrice) Peele's home, attracted 125 of 300 listed on Ruby Austin Burrus' charts. Cousin Albert (Bert) Austin, Sheriff of Dare County, acted as master of ceremony. Ruby gave the history, the current statistics, and presented prizes for the youngest and the oldest members present and recognized those who came the greatest distance to attend. I had the responsibility for the short memorial service, in which I read the names and their relatedness to the original family of those who had died since our last reunion. After a shower, we enjoyed food bought by the members and the fish that our hosts had prepared. We enjoyed catching up with kin and wished the rain away.

Charles and I came home the following week to resume our tasks and prepare for our July cruise to Alaska with the Reverend Chuck Swindoll of "Insights for Living."

We were to fly to Vancouver, British Columbia, to meet our cruise ship on July 21. Even so, I managed to work two long days doing research before the day of our flight.

The "Insights for Living" staff kept us occupied during our cruising hours, with a schedule that included instructive seminars, worship, and entertainment. One evening, while two pianists were playing George Gershwin's "Rhapsody in Blue," the two grand pianos tried to travel across the stage as the ship rolled and we were grateful for scopolamine patches to ward off nausea. When we were sunning on the main deck one bright day, we observed the calving of an iceberg, when great chunks of ice broke off and slid into the water.

Our ship traveled from Vancouver, British Columbia, into Southeast Alaska along the Inland Passage, with stops in Ketchikan, Sitka, Juneau, and Skagway, and back again. As part of our on-shore adventures, we walked on glaciers, saw salmon jump the frames, and ate a few at a salmon roast. We visited the totem poles in Ketchikan.

Charles and I had made reservations at a hotel in Vancouver to attend the 1986 Expo, following our cruise. The Expo was to be the last world's fair in North America for several decades and the last time the Soviet Union and Czechoslovakia would ever exhibit. Expo 1986 was more successful than either the 1982 World's Fair in Knoxville, Tennessee, that Shirley Durham and I attended, or the 1984 World's Exposition in New Orleans.

After the cramped quarters of the cruise ship, we should have enjoyed our spacious accommodations, but we were wearier than we realized. The next day at the fair, whose theme was transportation, we saw all we could and rode the Monorail and Skytrain to the exhibits spread over 175 acres. However, on the second day we arrived at the gate to discover we had left our tickets at the hotel. We were too tired and apathetic to retrieve the tickets and return to the fair. We went back to the hotel to wait for my cousin Barbara to drive from Seattle to Vancouver to pick us up the next day. We visited her and her friend Tex for two days in Seattle before flying home.

Work related to the litigation and pharmacy relief work kept me busy for the rest of the year. Charles was enjoying using his artistic talents to make signs and sketches for the church bulletins. I wanted him to enjoy his accomplishments. However, he seemed jealous of the attention others gave me and I cringed when he declared, "You intimidate me!"

I did not want to be a threat to him. I asked him to go to a marriage counselor with me. He refused, because, he said, "Julie and I went and it did no good."

We received an invitation to attend the Durham County Hospital pharmacy staff Christmas party at assistant director Bill Martin's home. Gerald Stahl, the director, asked if I would be willing to come back to work at the hospital. Happily, he was able to convince the administration to give me my old pay rate.

CHAPTER

{ 11 }

Charles received several messages from his family in January 1987 to cause him anxiety. Veronica wrote that she was out of money. While he disbelieved an earlier claim, he believed her now. With only his retirement, he could not help her. His grandson Paul called to tell him that his little sister Becky had an operation to remove a growth from her neck. On January 24, a message said his mother would return to her apartment the next day, after a light stoke and a three-day hospital stay. When I asked about his mother, he accused me of "digging and digging." He said, "I don't do that with your family. You're not to do it with mine!"

My concern for Charles and his mother was natural. However, his attitude became abusive and antagonistic and he moved into the other bedroom.

William Blake's (1757-1827) quote: "The bird has a nest, the spider a web, man friendship."

Friendship is as vulnerable as a nest perched on a tree limb or a spider web strung across an opening. Some unsuspecting person may destroy either, without intending injury. It takes mindful, vigilant, caring people to avoid areas where nests are built and webs are spun. I have inadvertently unsettled a bird's nest or unhinged a web by clipping a hedge or walking a garden path at night; injured a friend by a misunderstanding. I do not understand Charles' reactions.

When Charles left to go to his mother next day, he was angry because I called Lorrell to see what she knew about her grandmother. He locked himself in the car and would not say goodbye or let me tell him goodbye. He angrily called me an ugly name.

Hurt and indignant, I yelled, "I am not! Your treating me like one does not make it so!"

I was furious, but I excused his behavior because I suspected that he was apprehensive about his mother's illness and his drive to New York. I discussed it with God: *God, do you really expect me to go on taking this kind of treatment from this man who promised to love and cherish me? Without your grace, I cannot. Lord, I can survive with hope, but what can I expect from this day forward? You are able, but he is a stubborn, angry man. You will not violate his will. Is he sorry? ... He was wrong to leave as he did. It hurt very much.*

Charles did not call me, so I called Lorrell. He arrived safely, visited his mother, and stayed overnight with Lorrell and her in-laws.

My friend Betty Moody's dad would have concluded, "He needs tilling to get to the bottom of it!"

How could I "till" the hard ground of Charles' heart?

He returned from New York but he would not look at me. Nor speak to me! That week, his boss at Becton and Dickinson complained that he took too long at a job. The criticism unnerved him. He spoke of quitting his job as a machinist with Becton-Dickinson. I wanted him to stay. I knew that working at his profession was good, for being back at mine helped me in more ways than monetarily and I was planning to ask for a permanent position at Durham County Hospital.

His mother's birthday approached, and he said, "Because of your relationship with her, you should go with me."

We did fly to New York for her birthday the first year we were married. That was nice. However, I had my job to consider. The fact that he had been talking of saving money so he could afford to leave our marriage and move to himself did not encourage me to accompany him. I should have gone.

About then, my son Andy's welfare became a big concern. Recently, a biopsy of the growth on his right forearm indicated clear-cell carcinoma. When he was a teenager, a growth in the same place proved benign. He did not suspect he had cause to be concerned when it grew back and delayed having it checked. To rid his body of cancer the surgeon needed to remove surrounding tissue as well. In order to save his life it might be necessary to amputate his lower right arm. Thankfully, when he underwent surgery March 24, amputation was unnecessary. However, the wound was very large and deep, almost to the bone. A graft from his thigh was used to cover the wound.

The infection in the wound on the arm failed to respond to a series of antibiotics, had still not healed after three months. His surgeon cleaned the wound thoroughly and took a new biopsy, but found no cancer cells present. Nor was the original source even identified. We thanked God for His mercy. After that, his arm and thigh healed nicely.

On April 17, Charles received a call that his mother had fallen out of bed and broken two ribs and was in intensive care. Tuesday morning I put Charles on a 6:30 flight, and drove to my 7 o'clock shift at Durham County Hospital. Charles failed to call to let me know that he arrived safely. To allay my agitation, I bought vegetable garden and flowerbed settings to keep me busy while I awaited his return. Two days later, he came home, and that night I went into his room to tell him goodnight. I leaned down to kiss him and he said, "Get your head out of the way. I can't see the TV!"

That hurt. Alone in my room, I cried and wrote this poem:

> *No, I won't feel sad or bitter*
> *I will trust God, Who can make velvet*
> *from a sow's ear if He chooses*
> *Almighty God loves me*
> *Anything He allows will not harm me*
> *Will only refine the gold*
> *Others have physical burdens*
> *Mine is emotional, inflicted*
> *by God's vicious enemy*
> *Nothing stands before God's power forever*
> *I will trust God, not my understanding*
> *I will sleep, Dream, love, live*
> *God will deliver me into joy*
> *I am His child/ He is My Lord.*

One month later, Monday morning, May 25 at 8:30 found us at Duke Hospital for Charles to undergo heart catherization. In the holding area, flat on his back, he was cautioned to keep his right leg perfectly still. He joked and laughed with his captive audience and claimed he enjoyed the whole experience with the nursing staff and Dr. Celestine Heavenly.

Catherization revealed that he had five blocked arteries, and his blood work showed undiagnosed diabetes. Bypass surgery, scheduled for Friday, could not be done until his blood sugar was controlled, so he was admitted to the hospital then. He urged me to leave, so I called my supervisor to say I would finish the shift he was covering for me. Work was slower than usual that evening and I was glad to leave early to come home.

On Friday, while I waited with others for the outcome of their loved ones' surgery, I reassured one very distraught woman. When they came to tell her that her husband's surgery went well, I was there to share her joy. However, I was alone when someone in scrubs came to tell me Charles was in recovery.

In the cardiac care recovery room, Charles had a tube the size of a garden hose down his throat and tubes everywhere. He had requested I take pictures to show him what happened to him while he was unconscious. I did that before I left him in their care.

Charles was on the respirator less than 24 hours and two days later hospital personnel were getting him unattached, bit-by-bit, from all the tubes so he could be moved to a regular room. He seemed depressed and irritable.

"Give me my glasses," he demanded, ready to watch TV.

Before his return home on Saturday, June 6, Charles received cards, flowers, and fruit from friends and family. Neighbors came by to chat. My sister Jo, who had been on Alaskan tour with her husband Carlos, called to inquire about his progress. Cliff, who was now selling natural gas for H&H Energy Management, Inc. in Wisconsin, called to check on his status. I called Debbie and Andy to let them know he was at home and to suggest a visit.

On July 14, 1987, his 91-year-old mother died. It had been little over a month since his surgery! Charles left for New York the following day. I took an early flight July 18, to arrive three hours before her 11:30 funeral service. Charles' grandson Paulie, Paulie's mother Jean, and his son William picked me up at LaGuardia.

At the service, in a tribute to his mother, Charles said that his mother taught Sunday school and took him and his sister Mildred to church. Later, Mildred said, "I don't know why Charles said those things about our mother. She never went to church nor gave to its ministries."

I was walking with two of his sons, Charles and Paul. I told them, "I can't deal with your father any more."

They seemed to disregard my remark, and I felt ridiculous. We gathered around the restaurant table to eat and when we finished we went to the lawyer's office for the reading of the will. I was there because I needed a ride back to his mother's apartment in Queens, where Charles and I were staying with his sister Mildred, her husband Ray, and their daughter, Renee. At the small apartment, Charles and I slept on a single bed with our feet in each other's face. Others were on sleeping bags on the floor of the living area.

Charles stayed to take care of immediate things, while I left a day early to return to work. Grief is a solitary place, and the loss of a parent is a difficult transition, emotionally and psychologically. When he returned, I knew he needed to talk, but he would not talk to me.

We had reservations for Prayer and Bible Conference at Lake Junaluska in late July. They were made long before his mother's death. Perhaps being with God's family at that beautiful mountain place would work a miracle of healing for both of us. My dear friend Joyce Dixon came from nearby Balsam to have lunch with us. She had recently had a mastectomy, followed by chemotherapy. Her hair had grown back though it was still short. My eyes welled with grateful tears of relief to see her looking well. Her husband Tom once said of Joyce to me, "If our marriage ever has a problem, it will not be Joyce's fault."

Her voice, her smile, her eyes, her touch are a balm. Charles responded to her benevolence. Surely, the interlude at Junaluska blessed him in his grief, but back at home, he wrapped himself in his emotional isolation, a sanctuary where he hoarded his grief lest I touch it or share it.

That October, we attended a Disciplined Order of Christ retreat at Camp Chestnut Ridge, near Chapel Hill. One evening, we were alone in a rude, outdoor theater at the campground. He smiled and said, "I plan to leave, but I think we should stay married for seven years."

Our marriage was less than five years old. I did not want him to leave nor believe that he wanted to go. I still hoped that he would consent to professional counseling.

After the retreat, Charles went to New York to visit his family and to attend to business related to his mother's estate. I flew to Wisconsin to spend time with my son Cliff and his new black Labrador puppy, a gift from his girlfriend Patti Schuette. His interesting Grafton apartment was located on the upper floor of what had been a factory or a warehouse. A river flowed by the building. While Cliff worked, I bonded with my "grand-canine," and cleaned up her accidents. I met Patti and her family for the first time during my visit.

Cliff asked if I would like to go to Glencoe, Illinois, to revisit the haunts that Don and I knew when we worked there the first summer of our marriage in 1947. Glencoe being not far away, we planned to drive there on his birthday morning and return to Grafton to cook steaks for our dinner with Patti that evening. However, we did not make the trip. Cliff and Patti had quarreled and he waited around all day for her to call. We celebrated his 31st birthday without her company.

Lee and I talked on the phone before I left to go to Wisconsin. He urged me to stop and see him in Kansas City. I could not do that, but I gave him Cliff's number and was happy when he called me there. Charles did not call.

After we returned home, I decided it was time to separate our belongings. I moved Charles' chest of drawers to his room and said, "Charles, I do not want you in my room anymore."

He participated that evening at Prayer and Share. We studied and discussed discipline as a means of spiritual growth and freedom; and the danger of our using discipline to repress uniqueness, rather than seeking to find freedom to express that individuality. The others left, we watched a TV program, and Charles asked, "What are you doing tomorrow?"

"Do I need to do something for you?" I responded.

He did not answer. Instead, he seemed angry and he huffed off to bed. Did I misread his emotion? Did his emotion cause him to misread my answer? What did he want? Did I miss a cue? Was he ready to see a counselor with me?

Lee wrote that while on his job at Wal-Mart, he had a verbal disagreement with a fellow worker. He became angry, which overstressed his circulatory system and he ended up on the floor. He was taken to the emergency room of Liberty Hospital and, on November 18, he underwent surgery to clear the carotid artery.

After Christmas, Patti and Cliff came to Chapel Hill for a short visit to announce their engagement. Charles and I took them to Slug's one evening for dinner to celebrate and I believe Andy and Debbie joined us. On New Year's Day, Patti and Cliff left us to return to Wisconsin.

CHAPTER
12

Charles helped Patti and Cliff pack up for their trip on Friday, New Year's Day 1988, which put him in the mood to call all his children, and so he did. I went to Cary to take Andy and Debbie some black-eyed peas from our ample supply of leftovers; and to give them a ride in the Cimarron, a smaller, cheaper Cadillac model, I had purchased. (I loved that car and drove it for 10 years.) Andy and I took Debbie to work at the pharmacy. Then we went to his office, located in a townhouse model. He was the onsite representative for Neal Hunt Realty at the time. He obtained his real estate license, while he was still in graduate school. He moved from maintenance of the apartment complex to the sales department of the realty company.

Cliff and Patti traveled as far as Washington, D.C., to spend the first night, spent a second night in Washington, Pennsylvania, and then drove 12 hours the next day to get home. They were so weary that they declared they would never make the trip by car again. I guess they never did, until they moved to North Carolina in April 1992.

An ice storm knocked out our electrical power that Saturday, and we were glad for the gas range and fireplace. At least we could cook and have hot water for baths, from the gas water heater. Charles went to work at Becton-Dickson, as usual, and I did my 1:30 p.m. to 10 p.m. shift at Durham County General. That night, we removed the bedding from our beds, laid them on the living room floor, and slept near the fireplace, our main source of heat.

The Friendship Notebook, with quotes by famous people, provided prompts for my journal writing. January 4, "Platonic love is love from the neck up." - Thyra Samter Winslow, (1903-1961)

Journal-*I'd enjoy a bit, not a glut, of youthful passion. Maybe it is a lost dream to one past 60. Or is it? I still need to give and to receive expressions of affection.*

Strangely, Charles decided to come back to my bed that night, but I was not pleased. One gets used to one's selfishness and prefers having enough covers to keep one snug and not being awakened by loud breathing.

Bad weather kept Mona, Bill and me from going to Richmond to attend the District Four Court of Appeals regarding the land litigation. Jo and Carlos went from Hatteras. Attorney McNairy represented the Phipps and Attorney Archbell spoke for us. Our niece Beth Williams once worked for J. Harvie Wilkinson III, one of the judges sympathetic to our cause, but the other judges were not. (It would be three or four months before we would have a decision. By then, we would have been involved with the litigation nearly three years.)

Soon after that, I received a surprise phone call from Charles Harris of Sun Realty to express interest in buying my part of the Hatteras claim. I could not imagine anyone willing to risk buying land under protest.

In spite of the bad weather, bad road and my suggestion that they wait for better weather, Eddie, Diane, Faye and Snow came a day early to celebrate Snow's third and my 62nd birthday. Andy and Debbie joined us for dinner. Eddie and Diane purchased Kid Sister, a doll as big as Snow herself, with Charles' gift of money to Snow.

Still not satisfied that divorce was the right course for Charles and me, I wrote to Billy Graham's wife, Ruth, who had her secretary write and send me Dr. Ed Wheat's wonderful book, *Love Life for Married Couples.* Dr. Wheat, a Bible and Greek scholar, gave background for the Bible truths he used to make his points. He said that anyone could use Bible truths to restore a failing marriage by commitment to love.

After telling about a case similar to ours, Dr. Wheat wrote that the two could not possibly work it out alone. Neither could we. We needed help or a miracle.

We were free to decide just as Adam and Eve. We had the same freedom of choice as the two in the Garden of Eden. I cared for Charles. I believed he cared for me, in spite of everything.

Our church Valentine event included everyone. I am not sure that I read the sign Charles made to announce it. If I did, I forgot what it said. When, on the night before, I asked him details of the event, he replied, "If you read my sign you'd know everything you need to know. I don't know why I bother to talk to you."

"Charles, please! Don't be so critical of me! You forget too! You got Red Delicious apples instead of the Rome."

"It never happened before!" he claimed. (It had!) "If you are going to criticize me, you can do the shopping yourself."

He got up from his chair. "Are you going to bed?" I asked.

"I don't ask you questions. You don't ask me any!" he said.

Nevertheless, Valentine's Day morning he came into bed with me and we went with the church crowd to Shoney's for Valentine breakfast. That evening, Andy and Debbie came for supper. After they left, he helped me clean up the kitchen. When he disappeared, my optimism plunged. I was confused by what had happened, for he gave me a loving homemade Valentine, came into my bed that morning, the Valentine party with the church family, and dinner had gone well. I wanted to love him and have him love me. My Valentine to him said, "Nothing enchants me like when you romance me."

Four nights later, he declared, "I am seventy-five percent sure that I want out of this marriage. I am looking for an apartment and will leave on our fifth anniversary."

During the discussion that followed, he spoke of how his employment had helped him to feel: "I am not just rocking back and forth," he said.

I was happy for the confidence it gave him. However, his description of himself as my "lap dog" made me cringe. I did not regard him that way! Nor had any dog I ever owned rejected me and been as unpleasant as Charles.

I decided not to argue, entreat, or seek to change his mind, even though his leaving would make my financial position more tenuous, since we split the monthly household expenses. He paid for his long distance calls and the cost of his health insurance, which was under my contract with the North Carolina State Retirement System, a benefit given to me as Don's widow. Charles' contributions helped. So I felt threatened when my work supervisor, Bill Martin, told me they were thinking to use the regular pharmacy staff to cover my hours and eliminate my position in April. I would need to be more frugal.

Journal - *Tension is high. How can it be otherwise, after Charles' announcement and his passive-aggressive behavior? He is congenial until he thinks I am on his side. He then retreats to be out of reach. He said that*

Julie divorced him for mental cruelty. He is cruel and cold! With ready tears for that which touches him on TV! I am more alone than if I had no husband. The breach between us causes me pain.

A woman speaker I heard today said that it is instinctive for a woman to be submissive to her husband. He accuses me of taking authority that he refuses to assume. I want him to be strong. I would be more secure if he were.

Journal - *Thank You, Father, for grace to weather whatever is to be. I would like to abort him quickly, to relieve the pain. But, I trust You, God, and Your timing. Who does he think he is to go against Your words to him as a Christian husband? Is he going to chafe against Your love until he must finally surrender? It is between You and him, God. It is Your business!*

The next night's entry: When *Charles started his insults tonight, I told him I had decided that he was right. I suggested we begin by trading his part of the shares of Orange Federal and Savings Loan stock, which we purchased together, for my Horizon, which he was driving. I offered him the Timeshare week, since we would not be going together. I pointed out that there were many places advertised in* The Village Advocate *that he might rent. His insults stopped. He became cordial.*

He has no right to an opinion in anything that concerns me after his statement five days ago. I am not furious. I am resigned - calm, cool, careful, controlled. But not contrite!

At work, I ate lunch with a young woman from our department who I found sitting alone. She looked sad, hurt, and angry. I asked if I could join her and if she needed to talk.

"No, I don't want to talk, but please join me."

We talked about a variety of things to divert her attention away from self-pity. After we had eaten, she asked if I would like to walk outside with her, and I agreed.

The day after Charles' tirade, as I added doctors' orders into the computer, I suddenly became aware of her standing beside me.

The light was back in her eyes. She smiled and said, "Thanks for yesterday."

"You're feeling better?"

"Much!" she replied, and as she walked away, tears spilled from my eyes. Charles' verbal attack the night before made me feel and half believe that I was valueless. Her words were like a balm to my wounded spirit and I remembered the Bible verse: "Bread cast upon water returns to the one who casts it after many days."(Ecclesiastes 11:1)

Someone walking by asked, "How are you today?"

"I'm fine! For all that I am sitting here crying," I said.

"Nothing's wrong?"

"No! On the contrary!" I smiled and repeated, "I am fine!"

Charles and I had purchased season tickets for Friends of the College (NC State University now) entertainment series, so one Friday evening in late February we went to Raleigh to attend the Alvin Ailey Dance Theater. The innovative dances and the colorful costumes and characters thrilled my sensitivities. I was happily surprised when the Ailey dance group performed on television that same week as part a tribute to Bob Hope with the opening of the Bob Hope Cultural Center at Palm Springs, California, on March 5.

That March, Andy and Debbie found a house they liked and put a thousand dollars in earnest money to keep it. I must have expressed my concern, for Debbie reassured me that her income as a pharmacist was high enough to meet the financial requirement for them to own a home. I was happy to make a gift toward their down payment and later gave similar amounts to each of the other sons – Eddie's as a deduction from his mortgage debt and Cliff's on his first home in Mequon, Wisconsin, later.

After a two-week stint at work, I made a car trip to Virginia Beach at the end of March to visit Beth. Jo and Carlos were coming too so we could celebrate Margie's 70th birthday, March 28. It gave me the opportunity to talk to Charles Harris of Sun Realty. I arrived early at Beth's to meet Mr. Harris. He had a proposal for the purchase of my Hatteras beach lot. By then I believed that he was ready to meet any price I might ask, but I was not convinced that I should sell. Our lawyer suspected Harris' company had made a deal with our opponents. (Andy thought we should develop the property ourselves.) I told Harris that I was not convinced, and he asked me to take more time before making a definite decision. When Jo and Carlos arrived, I was anxious for him to leave. We had more important things to attend — matters of the heart!

After I returned home, I spent a sleepless night trying to decide about the land offer. Sometime during the early morning hours, I rejected the offer (I cannot remember why), and I slept.

When Andy and Debbie moved into their home in April, they were expecting their first child. Debbie's labor began on a Sunday night and continued for thirty-four hours, with Andy by her side the whole time. Her parents and I were there for several hours, waiting and praying before the baby arrived. The doctor hesitated to give her more anesthetic for her pain because it affects the heart rate of the baby as well as the mother. She suffered far more than normally would have been allowed during a delivery. My first grandson, Austin Cole Skakle, 6 pounds and 14 ounces, was born May 3, 1988, at 7:46 a.m.

That new member came with his parents to visit Grandma Sybil's house for the first time the last day of May, and this fascinating, bright fellow received a silver-plated bank June 25, for being the youngest attendee at the Austin Reunion at Hatteras, which Charles attended with me.

However, Charles announced that he was not going to Cliff and Patti's wedding, scheduled for October 1, 1988. I had already exchanged our timeshare for one in Wisconsin for the week preceding their wedding. I told him, "I am going, Charles, whether you go or not."

He changed his mind. On September 24, we flew to General Billy Mitchell Airport, rented a car, and went to Cliff's apartment in Grafton, Wisconsin. When we rang Cliff's doorbell, Booker barked from the window above us. I spoke her name, and she stopped barking. Perhaps she recognized me from the year before. Cliff was not there and cell phones were not yet invented! We left a note for him and drove to Oconomowoc to take possession of our large apartment at Olympia Village Resort. When Cliff returned to his apartment and found my note, he phoned. I agreed that we would meet him and Patti the following evening to go to dinner at Mader's, an old German restaurant. Charles was German. That should please him. Not so!

"There is a political speech that I want to hear!"

Cliff said, "Tell him that I will tape the speech for him, so he can listen to it later."

Charles went to dinner with us. As far as I know, he never listened to the tape.

The wind howled that first night, and the rain was torrential. Charles moved upstairs and left me in the master bedroom downstairs, in a strange bed, feeling angry and insecure.

For the rest of the week, he had his agenda and I had mine.

I did not want to go horseback riding, and he did not want to go to the spa. Neither of us cooperated. Perhaps he did not enjoy his choices any better than I did mine. Given the years, I think we would have been happier had one of us been able to accept a plan for both of us.

One morning that week, we visited a farmers' market decorated for autumn. I took a picture of straw figures, dressed as a bridal couple, thinking that I would share the photo with Cliff and Patti, but I never did. Another day, I went alone on a tour of a house. Later, together, we visited an area close by our accommodations, just to walk around and pass time.

On Wednesday, I asked Cliff to come to Oconomowoc to have lunch with me. Charles agreed to my having time alone with my son. Cliff and I were eating on the porch outside the restaurant when Charles appeared on the ground below, but neither Cliff nor I invited him to join us. He took a picture, which I found recently, and walked away.

Debbie and Andy left their new baby at home with his grandmother Coltrain to arrive on Thursday. They decided not to take part in the parties that evening. After the 60-mile trip, to pick them up at the General Billy Mitchell Airport, we took them to the condo to leave their luggage. Then we went to Watertown to have dinner. When we got back at 10:45, I found a message from Cliff that asked us to meet Eddie at the airport. Eddie's plane had arrived at 8:45. When Cliff volunteered to meet Eddie, he forgot he had a bachelor party that evening.

I was baffled. Now what were we to do? I called Cliff's apartment and there was no answer. I called the airport to have Eddie paged, with no results. We drove back to the airport, hoping to find Eddie, but he was not there. Had he even come?

Finally, back at our resort, I called Cliff's apartment again. Patti answered. She was livid that she had had to pick up Eddie. She had her bridal affairs to attend. She threatened to cancel the wedding. Eddie had arrived, waited awhile, called Cliff's apartment and awakened Patti, who was exhausted and asleep. She went to the airport, picked Eddie up, took him back to Cliff's apartment and Eddie was now fast asleep. I awakened Patti for the second time that night. No wonder she was angry. However, after erupting, she stated that she had spent too many hours planning her wedding not to go through with it.

Eddie was still irritated when I telephoned Friday morning. "I waited four hours in a strange airport in a strange town!" he complained.

Charles and I made the trip to Grafton to pick him up and take him back to our resort. That afternoon, Eddie and Andy played golf. By evening and rehearsal time, Eddie was ready to enjoy the moment. Everyone showed up for the rehearsal dinner at a local restaurant in Milwaukee, which Cliff and Patti had engaged for me to host the rehearsal dinner.

It was fortunate that Charles and I went to the church where they were to be married on Friday. I needed to sign a statement for the young Catholic priest to attest to the fact that Cliff had never been married and was qualified to marry Patti. On Saturday morning, our guests and we had to check out at Oconomowoc and move into the motel at Watertown where we had made reservations. The morning was rushed. We grabbed some lunch, dressed, and made our way to the church to join the rest of the wedding party, with little time to spare.

The bride was lovely, the groom, handsome. My dress was mauve and floor length. Eddie walked me down the aisle in Andy's dark suit and his own tan Hush Puppies. During the ceremony, he read the Scripture; the pianist played the special music Cliff had composed for Patti; and the priest gave the Eucharist meal to all us mongrels, except Cliff's Jewish best man, Gary Taxman. (Milwaukee is home for Gary. His and Cliff's friendship goes back to college days when they played tennis under Cliff's father.) Andy and Debbie were in the wedding party and, when the wedding candle light kept going out, Andy persisted in trying to keep it lit.

Cliff and Patti rode in a white carriage drawn by a Clydesdale horse to the dinner and reception at the Renaissance, a building that once housed a Christian Science reading room. Its décor, quite lovely, was rose and maroon.

Truly, Patti's hours of creative planning, mentioned on Thursday evening in anger, produced a beautiful wedding. The ceremony, the horse-drawn carriage for the bride and groom, the sit-down dinner, and the band and dancing made a perfect whole. I danced with each of my sons in turn but do not remember that Charles asked me to dance. I do remember him for his kind understanding at the airport as Andy and Debbie, and Charles and I prepared to take our separate flights. Debbie said, "Sybil, relax, you have been taking care of everyone all weekend."

I mistook Debbie's remark for criticism and my face must have shown it. Charles said, "It isn't any wonder you are emotional. Your youngest has just married, you've just said goodbye to them, and your oldest son has just flown away."

Yes, it had been a stress-filled week. My reception equipment was full of static.

As I think, objectively, about that trip and that week, Charles was still grieving, and the year had been full of stress. It is a wonder he survived, considering his history of an earlier heart attack, a five-artery bypass, the death of his mother, and our unhappy relationship during the current year. However, I did not attribute his behavior to stress and thought it inexcusable. To use a childhood term, it seemed he was "cutting off his nose to spite his face." Sharing his grief would have strengthened our relationship and have helped him to heal had he been able to do it!

Back home after the wedding, I picked up the rhythm of my life again. The University Woman's Club group called Gems, meaning Generation in the Middle, was to meet and I persuaded my friend Margaret Ronman to go with me to see our hostess' charming little house in Chatham County. The little house became a metaphor for a journal entry that night: *I am Eve in the Garden wanting to know what God knows, to take charge. Fear and rebellion stand defiantly in my heart. I dissent against fleeting time and not getting what I want or expect. O God, please, help me get my "little house" ready, as our hostess did today, ready to receive the new tenants - Contentment, Joy, and Love whom You will send to inhabit the rooms of my being.*

In November, Adam, my sister Mona's son, and his wife Cat gave Mona a birthday party at Chapel Hill, where Adam was attending medical school at the University of North Carolina. Charles refused to go with me, but Andy and Debbie were there with little Austin.

When I arrived at a second party to which Charles and I had been invited, Charles was there with our pastor and his wife Mary. Charles was wheeling Mary into the door. "Hello, Sybil," he said.

I greeted Mary and Jim and said, "Hi, Charles," as I walked past him. I did not feel gracious toward my husband.

He brought up the subject of separation in the middle of December, but said, "I am not going to leave. That would be desertion."

I already felt emotionally abandoned and a note I found beneath a picture of us on the refrigerator did not amuse me. It said, "No regrets Charlie still a good tuna sandwich." Rather, my pent-up anger made me resent it. What did he mean?

On Sunday, December 19, Don's and my first grandchild, Stephanie Snow, dressed for the occasion, was the first to be christened from the new baptismal font purchased with funds given in memory of her grandfather. Andy and Debbie brought little Austin, dressed in red-figured pants with matching suspenders and a black bow tie. After worship, all except Charles came back to the house to eat the dinner I had prepared for this special day.

On Monday, I went to see my lawyer, Chuck Beemer, regarding a legal separation. He was sympathetic but gave no advice. Since we had a prenuptial agreement, the separation agreement presented no complications. After a year's separation, a no-fault divorce appeal would be filed with the courts.

That evening I told Charles, "You are you. I am who I am. Neither of us can change. Our differences are there."

"Incompatibility is the word," he said.

"I am sorry I failed you. I know you did not want it to turn out as it has," I said.

"It's probably most my fault," he said. "I saw things changing and made no move to stop it."

Your emotional neglect of me starved our marriage, I thought to myself, but I said, "Charles, I want to be your friend."

After working the day shift on December 23, I came home and found a note: "I have gone to think about us. I won't be around for a couple of days. Enjoy everything."

My reaction was part anger and part hurt, mixed with anxiety. Where could he be? Had he decided to fly to see his family in New York? It was Christmas Eve. Was he doing this to spite me? I replaced my wedding band with the wedding band Don had given me. I asked Andy and Debbie to let me go with them to her family's Christmas Eve affair.

Sunday, Christmas Day, I awoke in the house alone. I was ready to leave for church when Charles came in the front door. "Shall we go in the same car?" he asked.

"No, I don't think so!" I replied.

He arrived at the church ahead of me and stood by his car as I spoke to the people who were entering the church. Through the glass doors, I saw him leave in his car, but he returned just as worship began, found me in the congregation, and came to sit beside me.

Outside the church again, I said the words that had been running through my mind for the last 12 hours: "Charles, this was the ultimate insult!"

"I don't see why. You told me you were going to Hatteras. I waited for you to ask me to go with you. You didn't, so I decided to go away for a couple of days."

"Well, I wouldn't have left you without explaining! You knew where I was going."

He had been in a motel room, and sometime during that time, he met a man he knew who told him: "You are a selfish man!"

As he told me about the encounter, his chin quivered and his eyes were awash. "I thought George was my friend. It really got to me that he told me that. I know that you have said it."

Accustomed as I was to his love of his own emotions, I was untouched

"I would like to go to Hatteras with you," he said.

"No! I don't want you to go. You will never mess up another trip for me," I said, for I remembered all those trips when his ugly humor and explosive temper had spoiled them. When we went to see the foliage in the mountains our first year, he threw a tantrum about the route I took. He berated me, from Wanchese to Wilmington, North Carolina, because our hostess, my cousin Myrt, talked the night before about someone whom she knew and their situation. When we arrived in Wilmington, we went into a pizza parlor and had ordered pizza when he got up and walked out, leaving me there. Once in Chapel Hill, we had ordered at Shoney's when he got up and moved to another table. I canceled my order and left him to walk home, which was about two miles.

No, I did not want to have his company on my trip to Hatteras. Andy and Debbie had invited us for Christmas dinner. We went in separate cars, and Charles got lost going and coming.

It was spitting rain when I left Wednesday afternoon for Hatteras. I arrived at my cousin Myrt's at 8:30 and she insisted we eat supper. We talked until 2:30 a.m.

I planned to stay in my apartment at Hatteras, but I found Eddie's place closed up tight. I learned that he had borrowed money to take Diane and the girls to Canada for Christmas. I went to Jo's and, God bless her, she welcomed me.

The next morning, the sun, bright and warm, flooded through the windows overlooking the body of water in Hatteras called the Slash. The water reflected the sun's rays and I, who overslept, lay still awhile just to think and to be.

I called Charles on New Year's Eve morning. He said he was planning his usual celebration with lentils and herring in sour cream, and I remembered our first Christmas.

"I've asked Laura to pray for our marriage," he said.

"Charles, it will take more than prayers."

"I know. I'm packing a little at a time." He added, "Circuit City is having a sale on tapes."

"Is a sale on tapes more important than our marriage?" I asked and hung up. My ears were dull, my heart closed. Were the tapes about relationships? Did I miss something important?

In Hatteras, I went to the cemetery to place red poinsettias on the graves. Tears spilled over and down my cheeks. Why did I cry?

13

"Prayer burden is to keep us from making a mistake or to get us involved in others' lives," Charles Stanley said on the radio station I listened to as I drove from Hatteras toward Chapel Hill. Whether right or wrong, I was involved in others' lives.

When Charles and I talked, he became agitated and unpleasant. He refused to believe his disregard for my feelings damaged our relationship. He could not hear me. He could only express his personal anger.

On January 9, I put the title of the Plymouth Horizon in his name. He had found an apartment and, on my birthday the next day, I helped him load things into the car. "Maybe I can think things through. I'll be there for you if you need me. I'll go with you if you need someone," he said as he left.

Charles' apartment was at the back of a large, old residence on Dobbins Road. A porch had been enclosed and divided to form a narrow living room and a kitchen. His bedroom door was abreast of the entrance door. The small, windowless bath opened off the bedroom. One evening, on my way home from a meeting of the Durham Orange Pharmaceutical Association, I decided to stop by his apartment. I saw the light in the bedroom before I knocked. He came to the door in his pajama bottom and a Carolina T-shirt. He seemed happy to see me and proud to show me his place.

He turned off the radio - he was listening to the Carolina–Duke basketball game - and turned on the little Sony TV, which Cliff sold to him, to watch a documentary about Ronald Reagan. Tip O'Neill, Speaker of the House was speaking. "Reagan loved the people, and they loved him. His genius was to surround himself with men of means and men of mind."

Charles offered me refreshment that I declined. When I helped him put sheets on his bed, I found my missing blue blanket. It was okay. He left me some of his furniture and pots and pans.

During our discussion, he confided, "I've a luncheon date with Jim Hobbs. I won't discuss our situation with him."

"Why?" I asked.

"He has enough to deal with," Charles replied, meaning his wife's multiple sclerosis and church affairs.

"Yes, but he wants to help you. I do too! Talking does help."

"I'd rather talk to you," he said, and chuckled. "You're the one to talk to about our marriage."

I did not disagree. It was a bit late.

"It's easier to talk here," he said. "When I was there, I felt I kept failing. I tried, but I always ended up in the same place with you."

"Why do you suppose it is easier?" I asked.

"We are off your turf. There, I felt like I was on the tip of a pin. I'm not settled in here yet, but it's easier."

"I don't understand that, Charles."

"I don't either," he admitted.

"About the timeshare, Charles, we agreed that if you decided not to use it, I'd find someone."

"Haven't you been able to depend on me?"

"Not always. Sometime you let your emotions rule you."

"That was there. I've been frustrated."

"Charles, God didn't fail us. We failed Him!"

At Christian Writers' group Lib Griffin asked, "Why did you marry Charles, Sybil?"

After I came home that day, I tried to answer her question for both of us. I wrote: *His old-fashioned intention to woo and win me was flattering. Tall and handsome with thinning hair, as Don's had been, his eyes were blue as were my mother's Daniels family. He reminded me of my mother's youngest brother Luther. His quick movements, while strange to me, were not unattractive.*

I was lonely for male attention, and his admiration and his ability to say nice things and do the right thing, opening doors and pulling out chairs, were gratifying. He had nice manners.

His imagination! He called himself Sir Charles and me Angel Sybil. That was charming. And his gift of the little dancing girl in a red costume and the boy in a white cap and blue knickers was appealing. His letters in envelopes decorated with bright colors and references: an airplane flying into RDU; a map of the USA with North Carolina and New York linked. These had been captivating. His letters sometimes came in twos and threes, even four. There is nothing headier in human experience than to be in love and loved.

Christian with values similar to mine, he loved Jesus and believed in obeying the Ten Commandments; enjoyed church things and champions them, same as I do. It seemed that if we were out of step with the world that we were out of step together.

I respected and admired his great affection and strong loyalty to his family. I expected the same for our relationship. Our marriage should not have failed!

Since neither Charles nor I used our timeshare week in May, I traded it for a week at Peppertree Resort. Shirley Durham went with me to Atlantic Beach the last week of February. The winter beach has a charm of its own. We enjoyed watching the sea birds and the changing moods of the ocean; did several jigsaw puzzles and read. One day we went to visit my widowed cousin Mogieannah Brown in Marshallburg, a village northeast of Atlantic Beach.

I responded to one of the several letters Charles wrote me in early March to declare his loyalty to our marriage as follows: *The horoscope was interesting and probably humanistic. No one or anything needs to encourage you, or me, to choose our own course. We do! Not because we are Christians--not because we are in God's will. We choose from our own self-centeredness most of the time. I don't believe God's will is the nourishment of your soul! Nor do I find it is the nourishment of mine.*

God wants us to choose His will and with my mind I know that His will is best chosen. However, neither you nor I claim credit in that department. We have chosen not what we know His will to be from the revealed word and Bible accounts. We are guilty. We can deny blame, but we are guilty. Neither of us has loved the other as Christ commanded: "Love others as I have loved you."

I am in limbo. I am a ship without a mooring. God still has the north star in heaven as it was from the beginning, but I'm drifting without a course.

Yes, running away from oneself is suicide. Don't do it!

Charles appeared with his bags the morning I was leaving to go to Hatteras for Easter, via Virginia Beach to see my sister Margie in a nursing home and her daughter Beth. "Charles, I don't want you to go with me."

"I want to see Margie too. She and I are friends. If you don't let me go with you, I am going to go in my car."

His devotion and compassion to Margie touched me. Besides, Margie accepted him and seemed to enjoy him. He was charming with her. I did not doubt that he would follow me.

"Hi, Charles, I didn't expect to see you," Margie said when we arrived. "How are you?"

At Hatteras, we stayed with Jo and Carlos, slept in the same bed, in her only empty bedroom, but without physical contact.

Easter was March 26 that year and we went with some of the others to the sunrise service at the foot of the Cape Hatteras Lighthouse, which Charles mentioned later in a letter.

News from Kansas City: Lee had prostate cancer and, in an effort to arrest its advance, determined by the increased elevation of prostate serum antigen (psa), he underwent surgery in April 1989 and endured 45 radiation treatments. He asked me to come for a visit.

When my grass emerged, Charles showed up to take care of my lawn. Sometimes he came, mowed, and left without my even knowing.

The first two weeks of May were very busy - a first year birthday party for Austin, a visit from an old friend Anne Mayor, who came to attend our fortieth reunion of the University of North Carolina Class of 1949. I invited Charles to go with us, but when he came dressed in a blue blazer and out of date black bell-bottom trousers, I requested that he go home and change to his dark suit, because I was wearing a long dress. "I knew you wouldn't like what I wore," he said.

"Then why did you dress that way?" I asked.

When he had not returned by 7, Anne and I left. We missed the social hour, but arrived in time for dinner.

May 10, Mona called me at work about the Phipps' litigation. I agreed to meet her and Bill, who were vacationing at Hatteras, on Monday at the lawyer's office. Again, Charles was ready to accompany me, but I refused his offer. I left Chapel Hill next morning at five and drove through rain all the way to the lawyer's office in the Southern Shores division of Kitty Hawk, North Carolina. I arrived at ten and found Mona, Bill, and Ruby, my brother Shanklin's widow, now married to the Reverend Joseph Moser, already there. Roy Archbell, our legal counsel, suggested we submit terms of settlement to the Phipps, since neither side had found definitive evidence.

Our lawyer, Ruby, and Margie sold their lots. Jo and Carlos paid fifty thousand to hold on to what they claimed and retired from the suit. Only Mona and I of the six original owners held on like snapping turtles.

On Tuesday, May 16, I was with Mona and Bill at Hunter Haven, their cottage at Hatteras, to celebrate their seventh wedding anniversary. The three of us walked on the beach in the sunshine and, after lunch, I went into the village to see Eddie and Diane. No one was at home and after waiting awhile and no one came, I went to see Jo, who was involved in the 1989 Dare County Cemetery Project, part of a nationwide effort to preserve the history of our ancestors. I urged her to write the stories she collected as she researched.

Friday, I stopped by Manteo to give Eddie's check to the Dare County Tax Collector to pay the remainder of his taxes. Then I drove up the beach and stopped at Roy Archbell's office in Southern Shores to ask if our proposal of the week before had been accepted. There was nothing definite.

I arrived at Beth's home in Virginia Beach at 4:30 p.m. Beth came home sometime after five and we went to eat dinner. Then she and I went out to see her mother at the nursing home. Margie, hot with fever and her eyes dark and expressionless, was weak and unresponsive. The nurse said, "I am getting ready to put her into a whirlpool."

"No!" Beth said. "You are not to put her into a whirlpool. She needs a doctor."

Immediately the nurse went to call a doctor. The doctor confirmed that her vital signs were irregular and that she was in no condition to endure the whirlpool. Both Beth and I agreed that no heroic measures would be made to keep her 71-year-old mother, imprisoned in her twisted, useless body, to suffer more ravages of multiple sclerosis, her bane for 30 years. Beth requested she be kept comfortable and free from pain.

"Beth, would you like me to stay?" I asked.

"There's no need for you to do that. You cannot do anything here. Her service will be in Greensboro. She will be buried next to Daddy in Westminster Gardens Cemetery."

I went home Saturday morning, May 19, feeling I should have stayed. On my way to work on Monday afternoon, I stopped at Charles' apartment to tell him about Margie. As I left, he said, "Happy Anniversary!"

Sure! Why not? I thought. *There are many hurt, maimed, desperate people on the highways and byways of life like us.* It is better to be friends than to be bitter.

Wednesday night May 23, I found Beth's message on my answering machine. Her mother died at 10:30 that night. Margie's death left a huge tear in life's fabric. I called Beth. After we talked, I felt very vulnerable in the quietness of my living room. I called Lee. He said I might call him anytime, day or night. Kansas City time is an hour earlier than Chapel Hill's. His voice reassured and comforted me.

Friday evening, I went to Greensboro for visitation at Hanes-Lineberry Funeral Home. Jo and Carlos, Ruby and Joe Moser, Bill and Mona were already there.

Since I thought Charles would want to go to the funeral, I asked him to go with me. He indicated a reluctance to go, but decided to accompany me.

As we headed toward Greensboro Saturday morning, he began to berate me: "I'm going to tell people who you are."

"Charles, what are you going to tell them?"

He did not answer. I do not know what he was thinking. True, I was talking to Lee and to God, and it constituted a triangle of sorts. My three loves, of God, Charles and Lee, had me confused. There was nothing anyone would care about hearing. As far as I knew, he did not know I was talking to Lee.

Andy arrived at two o'clock as we were going into the funeral home chapel. Charles did not sit with the family, so I did not know how he managed at the funeral.

Beth had engaged the Reverend Dr. Joseph M. Garrison, who served as the pastor at their church in Greensboro Presbyterian Church of the Covenant from 1945 to 1969, to officiate. He read Scripture to show how God is, and how man is in relation to God; and Proverbs 31 in reference to Margie - "a good woman, who can find..." The only music Beth chose was her favorite, "O Love that Wilt Not Let Me Go."

Margie and Curt's Greensboro home, where they lived for decades, had been sold a year earlier to provide for Margie's nursing home care. Beth and her daughters, Bonnie and Tanya, had quarters in a nearby motel. Charles chose not to come inside to join the others after the funeral service. He sat by the motel pool, and as I write this I think I understand, but at the time my Southern sensibilities chafed. I was not properly grateful that he attended the funeral against his misgivings. Perhaps we may both be excused because we both grieved our losses. Neither knew what the other was feeling or thinking.

I consulted my psychiatrist, who did not think my relationship with Charles in the marriage endangered me mentally or emotionally. Had I been willing to trust that he or I could change, I think I would have agreed to reconciliation. I did not want to hurt Charles, but I was glad to be out of the stormy marriage. Lee's friendship was like food and water to me.

Sunday, May 28, after worship at Amity UMC, I went to Cary to care for Austin while Andy and Debbie worked. It pleased me that he acted happy to see me. That evening, after Austin was in bed, Andy and I talked of his father. "I wish he could see where I am now," Andy said.

After Don's death, I did not want grandchildren because he, who delighted in little ones, would not be with me to enjoy them. Yes, I wished he were here to watch Austin grow; to see Andy and Debbie's success, and to revel in their marriage, too.

Devaluation of the dollar and inflation make true gains rare. With real estate, any gain should belong to the sellers, who as homeowners paid for the home, as well as improvements, and are taxed every year thereafter for its added value, even the debt! The gains should be theirs. On May 29, I wrote letters to Senator Terry Sanford and Representative David Price to express my concern that capital gains on residences were taxed.

I decided not to mail a letter I wrote Charles in answer to an angry one to me. I did not need to defend myself. However, a couple of days later, when he came to mow the lawn, we talked about his letter. No one, psychiatrist, Charles nor I, knew to whom or to what circumstance Charles' resentment toward me belonged. *Could it be a step toward healing of his memories?* I wondered. He said his psychiatrist gave him a 10 plus. I knew that he was not yet okay!

On June 1, I wrote Lee that I wanted to break off our relationship. It felt good to put my hope in God. The next day the phone rang. Lee thought my reason was that Charles was back with me. Charles thought I was having someone here with me. Irritated with both of them and myself, I was ready to spend more time with a psychiatrist. *I am determined to spend more time with my writing and plan my life as a single woman. I am ready to "Trust God with all (my) heart; and to not lean on my understanding,"* I wrote in my journal.

However, I wanted that phone to ring and to find Lee there. The next night he called, coughing and feeling miserable with a sinus attack. "Pray that if I die before I wake, my soul will go to the right place," he said.

Journal- *When I tried to tell Charles about a call from his sister he said, "Write me a note! Am I the witch in this story or is Charles the black prince? He is truly agitated and keeps throwing curves to hurt me. Neither love nor anger changes his hostility. Lord, Enable him to find the way and to surrender and be free.*

Ruby and Joe Moser came for a visit and were in bed, when I came home from work at midnight June 6. They got out of bed and we talked and prayed until 2 a.m. because I had received disturbing news. My sister Jo had called me at the hospital to alert me to a serious situation at Hatteras. That morning, she rode with two sheriff's deputies to take Diane to Cherry Hospital, a psychiatric hospital in Goldsboro, after Diane went out of control and broke things in their Hatteras store and the house. Eddie followed them in his vehicle. He was awaiting their evaluation when he called me next morning. Diane was herself and when I called the hospital the morning of June 8, she was no longer there. The psychiatrists decided Diane's rage was justified. Eddie had called his former wife that morning, it was the anniversary of their marriage, and Diane had discovered him talking to her.

Neighbors, the pastor's wife, and another woman of the village cared for Faye and Snow while Eddie and Diane were away. It seemed reasonable to expect that everyone in Hatteras village knew what happened. I invited Diane to come and bring the girls to stay with me for a few days. I asked God to forgive Eddie and me, for I saw a similarity between his actions and mine.

Journal - Diane and the girls are with Debbie and Andy and I have learned that the plot is more convoluted than I supposed. Eddie and Diane are still unmarried, which means my four-year- old grandchild is illegitimate. I am angry and hurt.

Eddie has no right to judge Charles. He has gone back on his agreement about the apartment in the house and failed to make his payments to me. In spite of that, I had faith in his good intentions, excusing him because fishing is sporadic and he had the added expense of his family. Until now! Still, why does Diane want me to turn Eddie out of the house? It seems to me that she has been party to what he has done against me for the past five years. I fault him for failing to visit Margie, his aunt. She was so good to him; kept him as a little boy for me to work. My emotions are raw.

The next day, I went to Andy's and Debbie's to talk to Diane and was with her for two hours. However, after going down avenues of thought to dead ends and seeking the right path in the maze, I felt afraid and defeated. In spite of Eddie's monstrous actions, I did not have the courage to act harshly against my firstborn. I wanted to bawl him out, but that would not help him or Diane. They had to work it out and let God deal with their hearts.

June 14: I am in a position of disrespect with Lee because I am a Christian. Charles is angry with me because he feels I betrayed him because I attempted to speak to his therapist. Bankrupt in my ordinary life, Jesus is the center of my hope!

Two nights later, Charles came with friends Shirley Durham and Margie Clark to our weekly Prayer and Share group, and I had no feelings for reconciliation. Instead, I waited for Lee to call, even while worrying about our inflated phone bills.

On Father's Day, Robert Fetterroll, Charles' oldest son, called and wanted me to give his father a Father's Day message!

Love is not a feeling. Love is the highest aim of life, life's greatest challenge. Love sometimes requires action; sometimes waiting. Real love of God means submission to His will, which is not easy to discern, and reliance on Him. What should I do? What could I do and still be within the will of God? Circumstances unchanged, I thanked God for my personal tranquility. However, I no longer trusted my oldest son to act as my executor. I loved him. I did not like him. I made an appointment to talk about many things with my lawyer.

However, there is always the other Mediator to heed. John 14:11: "Believe me that I am in the Father and the Father in me; or else believe me for the sake of the works themselves."

Jesus spoke these words to His disciples and spoke them earlier to the Pharisees! Both camps entertained unbelief. Jesus taught that love is the whole law, love of God and love of others (Luke 10:27). To love God and others we must keep the Ten Commandments. To break one is to damage both relationships.

That week I received a letter in which he attempts to explain his actions and feelings. Charles wrote: *"There is a big part of you in me. My passion for you slipped gradually. Strong morals seemed useless. Without* my consent, an inborn contempt ruled me. Recasting the above can only be cleansed and healed by the renewing of my spirit with God's. The Psalmist urges me to respond to 146:2 – "While I live I will praise the Lord; I will sing praise to God while I have my being."

My sleep patterns have released many negatives and wrong anxieties! God hears our prayers. Take care of my angel. He signed it: At the foot of His cross, Charles, in love.

He wanted to go to Wisconsin with me to visit Cliff and then to the Disciplined Order of Christ Retreat. I did not want him to go. Finally, I consulted the Reverend Elizabeth Thompson Severance, whom Durham County Hospital hired as their first chaplain sometime in the '80s. She advised me to decide what was best for me. "You do not have to say yes," she said.

Events had me suspicious of all the males in my life. I doubted their integrity and mine. I opened my Bible to the story of David and Absalom, who betrayed his father. That was no comfort! Nor was David's lenience, which spoiled Absalom.

Journal entry: *Why should I feel guilty to put myself first? That isn't to say that I am self-sacrificing. I make plans to indulge myself, plans for Radford for DOC and for my trip to Wisconsin. DOC is to help me find God's will. Wisconsin is for love of Patti and Cliff - and myself! In October, I plan to go to Aqueduct Conference Center to a writer's gathering. I am fortunate to have the means to do these things and the health to enjoy them. I do indulge myself, because God is good to me.*

Saturday and Sunday, July 1 and 2, I spent with Austin - a break from all the other. Journal- *I enjoy watching him conquer his world. He has tenacity and dexterity. He spent 30 minutes with a magnet one day. His little fingers played the notes of his songbooks, and, when I tried to help him, he pushed my hand away.*

Amity UMC welcomed the Reverend Richard Vaughan, his wife Debbie, and their four sons on Sunday June 28. They would be with us for the next eight years.

Journal entry - *It was a treat to finally hear Lee's voice after several days. I want to see him because he is above Charles in my affection. If I am to know what I should do, I need to see him before January. I don't know what to do about the Hatteras house and Eddie, or if I will have a choice.*

July 3: *I signed my new will today and talked to Diane, who is in Canada. I assured her of my support if she wants to return to North Carolina. I urged her to correct omissions* (I probably meant a marriage ceremony). *However, I have only one certificate of deposit, not yet matured, left; I have wiped out my passbook savings; and owe $35,000 dollars. I cannot help materially any more than I have already done by providing the roof over their heads.*

Jo acted in character and came to Eddie's rescue to save the house, which he had borrowed against to finish his boat. Three months in arrears on his loan, he paid $1300.00, all he had. Three weeks later the bank had filed for foreclosure. My lawyer remarked, "You are certainly a loving family!"

After I came home from caring for Austin, Lee called to wish me a happy Independence Day. Lee and I do not always agree, but it is easy to talk to him. We respect one another enough to allow differences of opinion. That is certainly part of true friendship!

I felt listless and down the next day. My friend Margaret called; I received a beautiful letter from my friend Joyce Dixon; and I received a card and note from Shirley Durham, who came for a visit the next day. It was as though God assured me through these friends that He loved me. Then, one night when I was working at the hospital He would tell me so.

July 18, I drove alone to Radford, Virginia to be part of the National Disciplined Order of Christ Retreat, to benefit from Sister

Jeanne Hill and the Reverend Tommie Tyson's teachings on inner healing. They taught me: 1) another cannot complete me, because God created me to commune mind to mind with Him. 2) Holy marriage is abandonment of self to another, expecting nothing except the privilege to love. 3) I heard, "If they will not receive your love, they will leave."

It must have been vacation time, because the following week I went to Hatteras, intending to help Eddie celebrate his July 26 birthday, and I spent five days. However, Eddie was not there. Again, I relied on Jo's hospitality. We had good visits; shared deeply as we walked the surf. As I left to come home, she cautioned, "Leave that Lee alone!"

She voiced some of the anxiety I felt about my intentions. However, feeling on the edge of everyone's life made me long for a life of my own to claim.

Lord, do I need loneliness and aloneness? Am I shaped by them to conform to Christ's suffering? Forgive me that I rebel. Sometimes I ask," Who do you think you are, Sybil? Why should God consider you?"

Lord, I sometimes desire anonymity. What do you want of me?

Dr. Earl Somers once told me, "You do not always know you've helped someone. Others have told me that you have helped them."

I did not dare ask, but would have liked to know how he could have known that and who told him. While I treasured the sweet possibility that I had truly helped someone in my heart and mind for days, I wondered if he had only told me that to soothe my damaged psych.

No, I really don't want to be unknown. It is just that responsibility tires and tries my mind and soul. I search for a haven for my soul's rest; for peace that will enable me to hear God's voice above the clamor of my emotions; and the confusion of my thoughts. Help me, Jesus! Represent me before Our

Father God. Free me, from this inward battle, to be fully Yours and to want the path You choose for me. I should trust You more than I trust myself!

The next day, August 2, Charles came to cut my lawn and invited me to supper. He had said goodbye and gone out the door when I picked up the *Coastland Times* and read of Robbie Gray's death in an accident. His mother and father had been in my first church school class at Hatteras. I uttered a cry of anguish. Charles heard me, and came back inside to comfort me. We walked around the block. Was reconciliation with Charles what God willed?

Journal, the following week - *I had lunch with Andy and Debbie at Land Lubbers, Debbie expressed regrets at leaving Austin at day care since they have so little time as a family. They need time as a couple, as well! Austin will benefit if his parents have their needs met. I wish Don and I had made a more concerted effort to have our times together, because we forgot who we were before children and work. Then he was gone!*

I stopped to see Charles next day. I expected my letter telling him that our reconciliation was not possible would hit him hard. He said, "I expected you!"

We talked as we should have years before. He cried and so did I. I love much about Charles. I know that he will be okay, but he claims he still loves me, but this time he believed me when I said we were not going to get back together.

Next morning he came before I was out of bed and had a nap on the couch, while I ate breakfast and dressed. He came for us to split the Orange Federal stock certificates, giving him 94 and me, 93

Father, You are the Director! Explain the script, please. Mark our places on the stage. Give us our cues. Help us put aside our own ideas of how we should play our role, so we can follow your directions.

On the Sunday before I was to fly to Wisconsin to be with Patti and Cliff, our pastor gave an alter call and Charles went forward. I wanted to go but listened to the accuser of my soul: "You're trying to dramatize the situation," he taunted.

Did I miss my prompts and refuse to follow directions?

Journal: A day at work, two wrong turns as I drove, before I found the sales office of Ashley Forest, a new subdivision of New Fortis Homes, where Andy works. He took me to the United Airlines at Raleigh-Durham Airport and Patti and Cliff were waiting with flowers for me when I arrived at Milwaukee a little after eight o'clock that evening. Cliff brought me coffee in bed in their new home next morning and Patti took me to have a manicure. For lunch, Cliff treated at Ocean Cliff, under an umbrella with the sun at our backs. When Lee called me from Kansas City, Cliff said, "Mom, marry a rich man!" and he promised to find me one!

Their new home, distinctive and nicely decorated by its former owners, two gay men, included grounds with a large workshop and flowers and plantings everywhere.

The next day as we drove toward Wabena, Wisconsin to visit Patti's parents at their vacation home, Cliff did business for American Central Gas Company by mobile phone, which had a battery pack in a bag that he charged in the cigarette lighter. When reception failed, he stopped to call one of his natural gas consumers by regular phone.

The Schuette's beautiful home looked somewhat like a chalet, brown with white trim and a bit of black ornamentation. Two double glass doors, opening from the living/dining areas onto a wide porch, overlooked Robert's Lake and 403 acres of wilderness beyond. Birds were plentiful at the feeders!

I pulled up the colorful Dresden plate comforter that Patti's older sister Barb had made for their mother and snuggled down for another nap that first morning. The smell of wood burning awoke me a second time and I heard the melodious chimes of the clock at the foot of the stairs. How I did enjoy being there. I felt blest, except I worried that Cliff was drinking too much, in spite of his having spoken to me of his resolve to leave it alone. I knew it affected communication between him and Patti. At supper the night before, he had been on edge. Later when we watched their erratic TV, via disk and satellite, he seemed to relax.

We returned to Mequon on August 22, and ate dinner at a restaurant that once served as a brothel! Gary Taxman's parents, who looked as I remembered them from our sons' tennis days at Carolina, joined us just to chat.

After I returned home, I called Mequon and spoke to Patti. Cliff was in Houston, Texas. I wondered if he would find me a rich man there.

The next day, at the Carrboro farmer's market, a vendor said, "A good-looking woman like you should not be alone."

"Thank you! My son is looking for a rich husband for me."

"I'm not rich, but a warm heart and body are more important," he said.

When I told Lee about my farmer's market encounter, he said he was jealous.

August 30: My anxiety dream had me performing on a stage. I forgot what to say, was absolutely speechless, and the person behind the curtain would not give me my cue.

That afternoon, when I went by Charles' to thank him for doing the lawn, he was resting. I invited him to go to supper at Western Steer with me; my coupon would run out the next day. He seemed mellow, and I enjoyed being with him. When he spoke of a Christian mediator, I did not ask what he meant. He said, "I love you enough to want you to have someone, but there is no one else for me. I am a one-woman man!"

Do I love him? Am I sorry for him? He is working very hard to become whole and stable in his emotions, and I respect him so much for that. But is he to become a husband to me again? Do I want him? Would I let him?

When I don't know that I want, how can I plan a future? The prospect of reconciliation scares me. I am not convinced that it will work. What about Lee? He has been so kind.

When I talked to Lee, he said, "I've been thinking about you and Chaz. I think you would be smart to have options in case anything happens to either of us."

Maybe I will not want to share my space with anyone, but instead enjoy my solitude.

September 13 A letter from Diane prompted me to call her and we talked for more than an hour. Then I called Lee. He was too tired to talk, so I contacted him again before I went to work to see if he was okay. When he called that night, he was irritable and seeming to be itching for a fight, which was so unlike Lee! On the other hand, Charles came to the Bible study and left me a sweet note. He said I asked him to tell me how he saw me and he tried. Does he understand who I am or has he written what I have told him? I am grateful for the thoughtful, helpful things he has done since our separation. Can I trust that his anger has dissipated? I am glad that Lee and I have not met. Maybe God's plan is that we never will.

The next night Lee called but made an excuse that he was tired. When I called back later, he was listening to a replay of a football game. I felt disillusioned. Why did he lie to me?

September 18: We had been so busy at work in the IV Room all night that I had not taken my break. I volunteered to take the new fluid to the recovery room and then stopped at the small chapel, situated on the main floor near the elevator. When I walked in, one of the housekeeping staff, a young black man, stood by a table at the front. I slipped into one of three short rows, took a hymnal from the pew rack ahead of me, and sat down.

The man left. Then, there was no mistaking His voice: "Sybil, I really do love you." John 10:27

I looked down at the open hymnal to see these words: "Love Divine all loves excelling, Hope of earth to Heaven come down..." I began to cry.

Journal: *Lord, peace began when you spoke to me. I have been angry and rebellious for so long. Then you said you love me. The thought of Margie made me cry. I had not grieved for her. Perhaps I should - need to! I do miss her, miss seeing her! Yet to grieve seems wrong when death gave her all she lacked and wanted most - wholeness and freedom. Thank you for welcoming her home, Father!*

As I worked at the hospital computer tears came, from an ample supply, as I thought of Margie. Early that morning I dreamed of an old boyfriend, dead 33 years. Grief for him, coming so late surprises me. I thank God for tears and releases. Lord, my moral judgment sometimes impairs my love for those you love. Forgive me. Temper me and others by your loving chastisement and steady guidance.

September 21: Hurricane *Hugo*, a terrible storm, threatened the United States. It was due to come in at Charleston, S.C., and Charlotte, N.C. We had heavy rains, and the airport was flying planes from Raleigh-Durham to somewhere in Tennessee. I spent the day at Holiday Four Seasons Motel to earn six hours continuing education credit required to maintain my pharmacy license. Hugo lost strength when it headed toward Charleston, West Virginia. Charles came, cleaned up the debris from the storm, and mowed the lawn before I came home from Greensboro.

By noon on September 22, the sun was bright and warm. My friend Tillie Adams came to visit. Lee called to check on me after the storm and I called Eddie for Hatteras' status.

Lee called on the 24th and said he was planning to come to Chapel Hill for the November 18 football game I had mentioned to him. I am not sure I want him to come because of Charles. What am I to do? Wait? Yes, until *next May. Or, maybe it is better to let him come and to know, one way or the other. Either we really care, or we are only friends. Help me, Lord!*

It rained all the next day. After I had been home awhile, Lee called - I thought he would be asleep - and we talked for nearly an hour. Instead of going to bed, I sat down to play the piano, to enjoy the piano keys under my fingers and the musical sounds they produce. My talents are slight, but I thank God for the richness music gives to my life, for being able to hear its high and low tones and its sweet chords.

On October 3, Lee called to tell me that they discovered another nodule on his prostate, which would require therapy of some sort.

October 5: For seven and one-half years, we have corresponded. For the past seven and one half months we have relied on one another for support and encouragement. Now, I want to see him face to face - friend to friend. Love and friendship urge me, while considerations of propriety and reputation give me pause. Yet I feel I should see him before January 11, when Charles and I will have been separated a year, to know my own mind. A visit from me may help Lee face his bad news.

Charles and Shirley came to the Bible Study a few nights later. His visit to the hospital for a rectal biopsy had him completely undone. He deemed himself beyond God's healing hand. He was surly and defensive and acted as though Shirley and I were the cause of it all. We tried to reassure him and encourage him to trust God, but he was unable to think beyond his fear and left abruptly. (As I write, I see this as a revealing moment.) The next week, though depressed, he managed to vocalize his fear instead of acting it out as he had done the week before.

A book by Chuck Swindoll, our Bible lesson on purity, a tender letter from Charles, and my own thoughts all seemed to be persuading me not to go to Kansas City. A morning came when I felt I had surrendered my will to God and I called Lee to tell him that I would not make the trip. He did not protest.

During church that Sunday, the thought came to me that for me to go as a friend was neither disloyal to God nor against the claims of my life. However, the conflict between my heart and mind continued until I boarded the plane the following week, telling no one that I was going to Kansas City. I was too unsure of my actions to tell anyone where I was going.

Though legally separated for nine months, I was a married woman, a woman with misgivings about the flight to Kansas City, Missouri. I made my trip on my free days in the middle of the week so no one would miss me. My neighbor would think I had gone to see one of my sons. I trusted that nothing would happen in my sons' lives that they felt compelled to call me, because they would have no number to reach me.

The morning of the flight, I dressed carefully to bolster my confidence. I drove to the airport and parked at the curb next to Thrifty Rental, and took the shuttle to my airline terminal. I saw him first as I came out of the entrance from the plane to the waiting area in Kansas City. He stood waiting, but even though I had snapshots of him, he did not look as I pictured him. He glanced toward me, looked away. I walked up to him, smiled and touched his cheek. He smiled, opened his arms, and his big hug was our first personal contact.

He did not smile fully. *Gracious, what is that in his mouth?* I thought. *It isn't teeth!*

His hazel eyes were only slightly above mine. He was older, shorter, and had no resemblance to the Cowpoke I visualized and looked like no movie cowboy I ever saw.

After collecting my bags, we walked to his parked vehicle, a 1981 white, blue trimmed, Ford Econoline Van. It took exertion and a very big step for me to enter the van. Purple towels covered the front seats, and the dashboard held an array of medicines, crackers, pens, pencils - everything an emergency might demand. Two large antacid tablet bottles were in prominent view. Extra clothing, a blanket and pillow, a shovel, coat hangers, and an assortment of boxes containing other things lay on the floor behind the front seat. I saw a small plastic bag, which prompted him to say, "I don't put garbage in my trash at home."

He's careful, I thought, wondering where he put his garbage. Later, he deposited it in a supermarket dumpster on our way to his home.

"Barb teaches at the University of Kansas," he said. "I want to take you to a restaurant near there. They have a fine Irish stew."

We arrived and he came around to open my door to help me disembark. I felt shy and suspected that he did too. After our telephone conversations and letters, his physical presence was a bit overwhelming. *Was he glad I came? What did he think of me? How should I relate to him, as my friend or as my suitor?*

We sat at a table against the wall in the back of the dimly lit interior of the restaurant. He intertwined his fingers and rested his elbows on the table as he faced me. I liked his hands. We had practiced talking for the past nine months, so that was easy. He had listened to me sort out my feelings after Charles left; had been attentive and faithful with calls, cards and letters; had become my dearest friend, most-trusted confidant. Our conversation was pleasant and the food, good.

I expected a tour of KC, but he did not offer to stop for us to walk to visit his daughter. He confessed, "Sweetie, I'm not feeling well. Sorry! It's my sinuses. I've congestion!"

We drove to his home and he helped me take my luggage into his guest room. I followed him into his kitchen and went to the sink to wash my hands. He startled me when he warned, "Don't let water run in the sink. It isn't connected."

In the bathroom next to my room, I found many colorful towels hanging, even though he lived alone. *Maybe all these towels make him feel less lonely,* I thought.

I needed to rest since my morning flight had been early. I went into my bedroom and closed the door. On the back of the door was a picture of a nude girl. It completely unnerved me. I could not relax. I got up and went into the dimly lit family room, decorated in browns. The heavy gold drapes cut out any natural light, and no other light burned. Three TVs sat on the floor and Lee was asleep in his recliner.

He is like a mole in a hole, I thought. *I have no business being here.* I began to cry and sat down on the slanting cushion of a brown-covered love seat across from his chair. Lee awoke and struggled to lift himself out of his broken chair. He came to where I sat and put his arms around my shoulders. "What's the matter, Sweetie?"

"I'll take you back to the airport, or anywhere you want to go. Do you want me to take you to a motel?" he asked.

His second wife, Freda, died the year before Don. He had been alone a long while and needed someone to take care of him. How could I voice my doubts or tell him how discouraged I felt. I shook my head and wept. I would be more afraid in a motel than here in this strange town. There was no need to go back to the airport.

"Let me rest awhile longer," he said. "The pill I took makes me sleepy. Barb and Tom want to take us to dinner later this evening. We don't have to go. I'll call Barb and tell them not to come, if you want me to," he continued.

"No, no! We'll go," I said, straightening up and finally looking at him standing there in front of me.

Barb and Tom came and we went to dinner. Barb's beautiful smile, her warm and accepting personality, helped me to see how foolish my fears were. My panic was gone. These were my friends.

Until I told Lee, he did not know that his stepson had left the photograph of a nude girl on the back of the bedroom door.

15

On Halloween 1989, 31 years after moving into this house with a husband and three sons aged ten, six, and two, I came home, distraught, to an empty house. I called Lee. My department heads were discussing the elimination of my position and Lee was the only one I could bear knowing how scared I felt.

The next day when my neighbor Merle and I walked, I told her, "I'm thinking of asking Charles to come back to help with expenses."

"And pay it out in psychiatrist fees!" she said.

Charles and I had been able to talk recently. It seemed possible. Then he brought his grandson, Robert Paul Clukey, stationed in Georgia with the U. S. Army, to visit me while he was here to visit him. It was Thursday, November 5.

Jean and Willie, his youngest son, who had planned to meet young Clukey in Chapel Hill, had not come. A flat tire and Willie's open can of beer resulted in his arrest and Lorrell, Charles' youngest daughter, had paid the court fines. Now, Charles, highly agitated, made me the scapegoat for his anger and disappointment. Again, I forsook thoughts of reunion.

Jo and Carlos came for Mona's early birthday party to be given by Adam and Cat that evening. When they were ready to return to Hatteras two days later, I rode with them to join Debbie, Andy and toddler Austin at Hunter Haven. Debbie's parents joined us later in the week. Debbie wanted Andy to spend more time with her and Austin. Andy enjoyed spending time fishing with Eddie. Debbie's mother Ruby Lee and I understood! Our men love us, but they enjoy the company of other males for something we cannot give them. Men with men speak a different language. I suspect that women with women talk differently too!

One day while at Hatteras, I visited 86 year-old Oliver O'Neal with Jo to question him about the Slash, the body of water that divides the village. He knew it well and said that he had "skiffed" up and down it as a boy and an adult. We hoped he could give us a clue that might help establish property lines for the land litigation. Our visit, pleasant as it was, gave us no information to help us.

When I called Hatteras, November 11, after Debbie's parents had dropped me off at my home, Andy had disturbing news. Diane, pregnant, began to bleed, and Debbie took her to Elizabeth City to the hospital. Eddie was fishing in the ocean and Andy had child-care duty, I suppose.

When I talked to Eddie the next night, he explained that the placenta separated from the side of the uterus. They kept Diane at the hospital for several days and hoped the placenta would reattach itself. It did and her pregnancy continued.

While I knew Charles could not prevent my divorcing him, he said he would fight to keep our marriage. Lee's phone calls were a comfort to me and I was reluctant to end my relationship with him, but I was not sure that I should continue it either.

Journal: *My women friends with whom I ate lunch expressed the opinion that a woman is better off alone than with an ailing or depressed male. I am not a Florence Nightingale.*

"Get a dog!" one advised.

"A dog has fleas and needs care!"

"A cat?"

"I don't like cats!"

Animals cannot substitute for a loving spouse! I longed for human arms to embrace me and for someone to love. With a husband and corporeal satisfied, I could concentrate on the spiritual. Lord, you know me. You love me as I am. Thanks.

Jo and Carlos stopped by on December 15 to pick me up to go to Emily Graham's wedding in Asheville. I looked forward to sharing the family's joy. Emily's mother Louise and I were lifelong friends, and her father Bob had been Don's college roommate. Carlos was Emily's uncle. The family connections were numerous!

Getting to the rehearsal party at Grove Park Inn on the frozen, steep, ice-covered streets of Asheville was an adventure in itself. For the Sunday wedding, the bridal party members were dressed in Christmas colors, and the church, already decorated for Christmas, provided the background for the colorful wedding ceremony.

Back at home afterward, Christmastime included the usual activities with family and church family. However, I received three very special gifts that year. Terri Harrison, one of the black techs at the hospital, gave me a Mickey Mouse watch. We had talked about our Christmas expectations in the IV room at work one night and I told of wanting a Mickey Mouse watch as a child and of my disappointment when I received an ordinary watch.

Terrie said, "You deserve it. You treat all of us the same!" when I protested.

"Santa Claus already came for me! I finally have my Mickey Mouse watch!" I told my family that Christmas morning.

"Sybil, don't be too sure of that!" Debbie said as she deposited a big, gaily-wrapped package containing a Smith-Corona word processor at my feet. It did top my Mickey Mouse watch! The gold love-knot earrings from Cliff and Patti were small and costly. Truly, the gifts of this Christmas were the most extravagant I had ever received.

Since Cliff and Patti spent Christmas with her family in Wisconsin, the Skakle Christmas was postponed until Wednesday after New Year's Day. Eddie, Andy, Debbie, Austin, Cliff, Patti and I assembled to exchange gifts with Cliff and Patti, and to have dinner. Diane and the girls were not with us. They were living in a rental, a beach cottage, but apart from Eddie. Diane wanted to return to Canada.

Charles came and sat with me at the New Year's Eve Watch Night service. Together with the congregation we spoke the covenant, but my heart was not at peace. Did I really want God's will?

CHAPTER

{16}

January had some unusually warm days, one 71 degrees. Another thing I noted in my journal is that Attorney Archbell reported our opponents agreed to a 50/50 split to end the litigation, which neither hoped to win. Charles and I visited to talk several times during the month. There was tension between Lee and me when we talked. He was irritated and I was defensive. With God, I had peace. I decided that I could live without a husband, as long as I had God.

"Sorrow stretches out the space in the heart for joy," a quotation caught my attention January 18. God can bless us even by our sorrows and disappointments.

When Charles brought me a get-well card, because I had the flu, it included a note in which he expressed hope for our marriage. I had given him reason to hope because I had been unable to decide what I wanted. God would not overwhelm me with His strength. I was to use the free will He gave me.

February 3: *Charles came with a cardboard for a sign that we were to make with cut out snowflakes, to decorate the church bulletin board. And two mornings before that I awoke with three lines of poetry in my* mind: Dust to snowflakes/ Sinner redeemed/ God's loving miracles. Had I missed God's prompt?

Charles came on the fifth and left a letter with a check for his health insurance. Lee called and said his daughter Barb encouraged him to come to see me. He had made plane reservations to come visit. We needed to be together to know our hearts.

"Our narcissistic society has given us wrong expectations of marriage." Perhaps the radio broadcaster who said that is right.

Perhaps so! *I want to curl up like a kitten in the sun without fear of "dogs" disturbing me. I have gained 25 pounds; have lost security of my inner citadel. I feel bricks are being removed, one by one, to expose me. But it is not that I blame Charles. I do not love him enough to take another chance.*

My friend Margaret Ronman exhibits early signs of Alzheimer disease; accuses her stock broker of fraud; and cannot understand my explanations. She and Mike need help.

Charles brought me a silk flower in a clay pot with a homemade Valentine, signed: friend, when he came to Prayer and Share.

After I had picked up Lee at the airport and we were home, he stopped me at the hall doorway. "Sweetie, I can't ask you to marry me. With prostate cancer, my future is too uncertain."

We stood and looked into one another's eyes. "We'll talk about this later," I said.

This was his first visit to my world. We did many different things while he was here. Charles still did not know about Lee so I was a bit guarded. I told him about wanting to come to see him and attend the United Methodist Women's World Assembly that was meeting in Kansas City. I took him to visit my very dear friend Closs Wardlaw. The time went fast and he was gone. We did not know what the future held for us.

Back home, he was faced with the decision between radiation or removal of the prostate by surgery. He wanted to get a second opinion, but whether he did or not, he chose radiation instead of surgery.

In March, I began in earnest to master the mysteries of my new word processor, which made corrections so easily! Copy and paste made editing fun, an adventure of sorts. With my productivity greatly increased, and clean copy, I began to receive positive results from my submissions of poems and stories to various publications.

The young pharmacist, whose hiring had threatened my job, left the hospital the last of 1989, so I was still employed. After a week of work and the weekend with Austin, I entertained my monthly bridge group the following Wednesday. Early Thursday morning, I took Margaret and Mike (Ronman) to the hospital for their doctors' appointments, as I had promised. That afternoon the Christian Writers met at my home. Of course, I was stressed!

Who will believe my innocence if Lee comes to stay with me? With God love is paramount and each individual is worthy. Does it matter that I am misunderstood? "Christ made himself of no reputation; and suffered death for my sake." (Philippians 2:7 KJV)

Lee insists that he wants to be here with me. His being here would give me someone to love and care for every day. He called the middle of March with terrible pain in his shoulder. He thinks handling carts at Wal-Mart caused it. "I thought I was going to die," he said.

"Are you ready?"

"I don't want to go now that I have you," he replied.

"I would be sad, Lee. But are you ready to face God?"

"He can take me if he wants to," he said.

"May I pray for you?"

"Yes,"

My eyes were wet with tears at the thought of losing him. When I finished the prayer, he said, "Thank you, Lord!"

Saturday, I attended a seminar on divorce, which was no comfort. That evening Eddie called, happy that his family was together and that Faye's schoolwork was improved. Five-year-old Snow was doing well. Some of Lee's news that evening was not good. His PSA reading went from 167 to 233, in spite of his radiation treatments. His good news was that he went to Mass.

The UNC Educational Foundation dinner is a yearly event. The Don Skakle Scholarship in tennis is one of those given to a worthy tennis athlete. I went alone because Debbie was ill and needed Andy to be there with Austin. I interact with the tennis players, coaches and other who give, catch up with friends within the faculty and the community at large. Going alone is okay. However, I enjoy having one of Don's sons or one of their families attend with me, if possible.

The next week I went to Washington, D.C. with the Carrboro Garden Club. It is no wonder I was weary and blue and that my prayers lacked direction and fervency the following week. I argued with God, blamed him, and asked for forgiveness in the same breath. My sister-in-law, Ruby Moser, called April 13, and I felt better after we talked and she prayed for me.

Journal: *Charles is very much on the scene, but unaware of how the scene has changed. He is faithful at the weekly prayer group. He tried to repair my refrigerator of its strange noise. He still keeps my yard. I cannot bear to tell him of my plans to visit Lee and to go through with the divorce. I hate to hand him another failure. I care for him, but I do not love him as a wife loves a husband. No wonder I feel guilty and that my prayers hit a brass ceiling.*

My life is like a knotted piece of crochet, which cannot be unraveled. My relationships with Lee, Charles, my sons, their wives, and a friend are tangled. The Hatteras property is part of the mess. I cannot correct the errors or start over and I am trying to figure out how to finish the piece. But how can I make it right?

Lee called. He had been to church again. He said, "I love Jesus and I love Sybil."

Mona and I wanted to meet with Terrell Smith and Tim Midgett, who were the representatives for the partnership that we formed to develop the Hatteras land. On April 17, I drove to Hatteras to join Mona and Bill, who were already visiting their cottage. Smith represented the Phipps and Tim Midgett, our interest. Midgett Realty, his family's company, had purchased our brother Shank's share from his widow Ruby. They met with us at the cottage and we told them of our decision and asked to be released. We did not discuss terms of dissolution then, however.

The same day I arrived, Jo and Carlos left Hatteras to take their oldest son Ken to Duke Hospital for an operation on an ankle, one of many he endured in his lifetime as a victim of genetic disease in which his bones thickened instead of lengthening as he grew, accompanied by arthritis as he grew older.

I was back at Chapel Hill the following Friday and Charles came by the house before I went to work. Saturday afternoon, I stopped by his apartment as I came from work and invited him to dinner with me at Golden Corral (where Breadman's is now located in Chapel Hill). I would tell him then what I intended to do. That evening, we ate and he helped me shop for groceries. We also picked up a prescription for him and had yogurt before I took him to his apartment. He looked handsome, but that was not the reason I failed to tell him of my decision to go through with divorce, discuss his last letter, or to tell him of my plan to go to Missouri to see Lee and attend the United Methodist Women World Assembly.

When I confessed my cowardice to Lee, he did not express anger, but puzzlement. I puzzle myself!

April 23 I attended worship and shared dinner and fellowship with my church family to commemorate the founding of Amity UMC 32 years before. That afternoon, after a nap, I picked a bunch of irises from my garden to take to Ken at Duke Hospital. Jo and Carlos met me there and the three of us ate dinner at Land Lubbers. Afterward, we drove to Cary to visit Andy, Debbie and Austin.

April 25: *Lord, I rely on Jesus' advocacy. I do not deserve to be heard. I cannot desert Lee in this time of his life. Nor am I able to cut Charles loose, or decide to be alone. No one can tell me what to do. I won't listen! Fit my way to Your will, please, God. Or, somehow fit me to Your will. Forgive me!*

The 13th Assembly of the United Methodist Women, with the theme "Witnesses for a New World," met in Kansas City, Missouri May 3-6, 1990. A member of Amity United Methodist Women since 1959, I served as a Durham District officer for eight years. Attendance at the assembly gave me a reason to go to Kansas City. When I failed to qualify as a delegate, Lee found a way for me to attend. A woman he worked with at Wal-Mart, a United Methodist Woman, invited me to go with her and the others from Liberty UMC to serve as an usher.

United Methodist Women's concern for the needs of women and children of the world keep us constantly seeking ways and means to improve their lives in affected areas, i.e., environment, justice, poverty, employment, etc. The gathering, larger than I could have imagined, drew women witnesses from all over the world. We ushers were stationed up in the bleachers but had an opportunity to go to the floor below to see the exhibits.

Except for the two days I attended the assembly, Friday and Sunday, and for May 3, I was at Lee's home cleaning and straightening, while he worked at Wal-Mart. On May 3, we went by car to Independence, Missouri, to tour the Harry Shipp Truman Library, but scratched going to Leavenworth.

During my visit, Lee and I talked a lot and were happy to be together. One day we entertained Tom and Barbara for lunch.

I found I was content to be there with him, but back at home, I examined my choices anew. *He's nine years older than I and will be 73 in June. His health is poor. He has had an intraocular transplant, a carotid artery clearing, prostate cancer radiation therapy, and castration. Why should I consider a liaison? All Lee is able to offer me is a loving, caring heart and companionship. Is that enough? My head says, "No!" My heart says, "Yes!" He moves me deeply. I want to take care of him, make his life sweeter, less lonely. His care of me seems as real as mine for him. There were more pluses in 1982, more to harvest from the spent fields of our lives than now.*

I have written a strange chapter to my life this year. I have disregarded my reputation to show concern for Lee and have found a deeper understanding of Christ's love for me. Do Jesus' words "inasmuch as you have done this for another you have done this for me." (Matthew 25:40) justify my behavior? I have changed.

Eddie phoned May 14, 1990, to announce the birth of a baby girl, who weighed eight pounds and two ounces. Both mother and baby, Chanel Brooke, were well. He was present at her birth in Canada, and observed the episiotomy to release the baby's head. He declared, "I'm in love all over again!"

They had married two weeks before her birth, April 30, 1990, in Elizabeth City, N.C. They spent that night with Beth at Virginia Beach on their way to Montreal for the baby's birth.

I prayed their new happiness would grow into a lasting, harmonious union, and produce a peaceful, happy home for them and their children, Faye, Snow, and Brooke.

When I talked to Charles about changing his car insurance and his health insurance, he was adamant. He did not understand that divorce would make him ineligible for coverage under my policy. I could change it without his signature, but I needed his cooperation to change the car title into his name. He said, "I'm giving up the car. God gave me legs!"

When Lee broached the subject of marriage again on May 21, he was unhappy with my response, but I had anxieties. He wanted me to go to Missouri. I like North Carolina. Would he blame me that he could not function sexually? Might he resent that my assets were larger than his? Would I? Psychologists say money equals power in a marriage. Is it possible that we might equalize our disparities somehow?

The day I went to have my lawyer finalize the divorce papers and to change my will was the seventh anniversary of my marriage to Charles. Charles had said that we should stay married seven years. It took only 15 minutes to tell my attorney how I wanted my will changed. The prenuptial agreement simplified the divorce process, except the Easter trip in March extended the date of our legal separation to April.

Two evenings later, I cared for Austin for Andy and Debbie to attend an awards dinner in Winston-Salem, May 23. Andy received recognition as the second highest yearly sales achiever for Fortis Homes. While at their home that evening, I read an article in *Clinical Pharmacy* which encouraged me to hope that Lee's prognosis might give him two, three, or maybe five years!

Charles brought his laundry to my home the next morning and I bleached his dingy undershirts snowy white. He was still with me when my attorney phoned me to come and sign my two legal documents. As I left, I gave Charles a copy of a letter I had mailed him earlier to confirm that our divorce was imminent. I agonized as I imagined his hurt and confusion. I hoped he would see his psychiatrist again and reread my letter before the divorce papers were filed the following Wednesday.

That evening I wrote in my journal: *There is no condemnation in Jesus; (John 3:17) yet my vows and the injunction:" What God hath joined let no man put asunder" condemns me. My feelings fluctuate between gratitude for God's forgiveness and guilt.*

As Mary Magdalene must have done, as she washed His feet with her tears and dried them with her hair, I spent a sweet time on my knees before Jesus. He accepted her. He accepts my praise and my imperfect love. In my imagination, I felt the touch of his hand on my hair and the affirmation of his love. The writer's insight concerning Magdalene in Jesus Christ, Superstar *seems plausible. The need to touch and to be touched is part of our sensual natures and is meant to bless us and others. How could Magdalene understand Jesus' love for her and hers for Him? How could she show her love for Him who asked nothing of her?*

On June 13 the divorce papers were finally filed. The delay may explain why Charles kept showing up at my home. He may have thought I had changed my mind. When I called him on June 19, he said he had been summoned to Hillsborough. He protested, "It was a trial separation!"

"Not for me, Charles! Not when you moved out of my house." Poor Charles! While Lee gave me the attention and support I craved and needed, Charles thought the physical helps he did for me made him a good husband to me.

When I arrived at Hatteras, having stopped to see Myrt in Wanchese for a couple of days, I planned to stay at my apartment, even though Mona and Bill invited me to stay with them at Hunter Haven. When I went into the house, Eddie was talking on the telephone to someone about the suspension of his driver's license for DWI. Another surprise was that he and Diane had bought a house in Manteo, having rented their Hatteras living quarters for $450 a month to someone who would move in on August 1.

Diane, out of sorts, refused to let me hold Baby Brooke. It was Saturday, June 23, the day of the Austin Reunion. She would not agree to attend, or for Eddie to bring the older girls. Andy, Debbie and Austin were there for the event which followed the usual plan, memorial service, food, and fellowship and sharing.

Sunday evening Eddie's family, Andy's and I went to dinner at the Channel Bass Restaurant. Eddie told us that he had to go to Elizabeth City next day for an alcohol evaluation. Eddie picked up the tab.

One morning while I was at the apartment, Diane and Eddie brought me letters which they found in the attic from Don, before our marriage. Other letters they found were those from a pharmacist mate in the U. S. Coast Guard on Hatteras Island, circa 1943-44. I had dated Virgil Purcell a few times and enjoyed his letters more than his company. Strangely, I became a pharmacist and now his letter about treating a sore throat with sulfa had more meaning. Penicillin was not yet available.

Back home, I found Charles' letter, releasing me from my vows:

Dearest Sybil,   *"Beautiful" June 24, 1990*

Thank you for letter & Post card. In total shame!!

Hoped and prayed that your trips and your stay in Hatteras was fruitful. It does take special time to share and care! Bless you in all these endeavors! It does make one stronger to evangelize and share another's burdens! Joys too!

Now, it's my turn to do the right thing for you!

Happiness is based on mutual giving! Strengthen this belief in me now! I must be content to judge your wisdom! I will not delay your legal action of divorce against me!

Perhaps I don't know what love is?! I failed you in failing myself. So, Charles tumbled down! It's a terrible thing and embarrassment what I did to you. My soul is kneeling because of it! I broke the heart of someone who loves me!

The hardest thing is learning some things about myself that I didn't desire especially to know! Growing can be painful! No pain! No gain!! Vows made at the altar and to you continue to dominate me. I love you more now! This significant factor shapes me to be a giving husband, even if it's hindsight!

God has reconciled us to Himself! He has given us the ministry of reconciliation! His abundance too makes up for some shortage! I guess not in my case! Yet, Revelation 21:5 "Behold, I make all things new." I have to accept the certainty that God can change human nature! Most of us can probably look back on victories God has won in those around us!!

Accepting that God can change human nature can give a new vision of ourselves and those near & around us. So, my heavenly father gave me this kindness and understanding to release you from your vows to me! Wisdom too!

And so the rains will fall! Consolation follows! Forgive me again!! God is love! "And to know the love of Christ, which passeth knowledge, that you may be filled with all the fullness of God!" (KJV) Ephesians 3:19.

Faithful Charles/with love always!

The court date for our divorce was delayed. On July 20, when I was unable to reach Charles by telephone, I went to his apartment. He was not answering his phone; he thought the divorce already final. We talked, I wept, and Charles had tears in his eyes. I told him, "Charles, I don't feel guilty as far as you are concerned. You earned the divorce. But I am guilty before God."

"You're right! I can't deny I deserve it!"

When I told Lee, he asked, "Are you sure you want to go through with this?"

"No, I'm not sure. I feel guilty giving up on my vows!"

However, when July 26 arrived I went to court in the old post office on Franklin Street in Chapel Hill. Charles did not appear to protest. Attorney Chuck Beemer held the Bible, swore me in, and asked the questions I needed to answer. It was over in five minutes. My marriage of seven years, two months and five days to Charles André Fetterroll ended, and I still had 20 minutes left on the parking meter.

I wept as I drove home, pulled into the driveway, opened the door, and stepped out of the car. My neighbor, Dirk Spruyt, came over to me by the car, "Are you okay?" he asked.

"Yes. Thank you, Dirk." My eyes were probably red.

I was unable to reach Eddie to wish him a happy birthday. His birth made me a new mother! On this, his forty-second birthday, another painful ordeal left me a woman of divorce. Birth wrenches the flesh and divorce, the heart!

The weekend was mine to care for grandson Austin, who now talked more and knew what he liked and wanted. He especially liked to watch *Who Framed Roger Rabbit,* a video tape, which I considered too violent. He became more hyper after watching the Disney characters, residents of Toontown! Definitely adult fare, with sexy overtones, the heroine Jessica marries Roger Rabbit because: "He makes me laugh!"

I felt about Lee the way Jessica did about Roger Rabbit: "He makes me laugh." I did not want Lee to be lonely. I did not want to be lonely!

When I came home Saturday after having been with Austin all day, I saw that Charles had mowed my lawn, picked up my paper, and hung the garden hose. Was he doing penance? Did he not know that we were divorced?

My friend Anne Cole, who headed Amity's education committee, urged me to stay when I questioned whether my status as divorcee disqualified me as a church school teacher. Later, Roger Shumate, church school superintendent, urged me to stay too. Robbie Vaughan, our pastor's oldest son, said, "You remind me of another nice lady who had a dog I liked."

I loved the children; they loved me. I enjoyed teaching them the Bible stories. I stayed.

Lee had good news from his blood tests August 3. The doctor said, "Remarkable! Both factors, acid phosphate and prostrate serum antigen, are down. Very low!"

Lee arrived Thursday, August 15, for the weekend. We made a trip to Black Mountain, attended church there on Sunday. That afternoon we drove through the Reverend Billy Graham's hometown of Montreat, on our way to the Blue Ridge Assembly for Lee to see where I had expected him in 1982. We saw Chimney Rock and had dinner at The Coach Inn next door to our motel. On Monday, after breakfast at Huddle House we went up on the Blue Ridge Parkway and stopped at the Folk Art Center. We ate hot dogs on Mount Mitchell.

Journal - *He is disappointed that I am not happy about the pretty ring, which he said he got for free, that he wants to give me. Is my reluctance due to the cheap ring or that by accepting it I may be leading him to expect more than I am prepared to commit? He's sweet and kind and would be a good companion, but never a lover! There are other inequities of age, money, and religion. Do I love him enough? Would he try to manipulate me by silence and peevishness? Fantasy is more romantic than reality. I am disgusted with me!*

That which excites me is the acceptance of my story, "Early Morning Appointment, by The State Magazine and that I am writing.

August 24 - After I received a note from Ed Brecht saying that he was dying, I phoned my friend, my college teacher, my mentor. I called a mutual friend, whose husband, like Brecht was retired from the UNC Pharmacy School faculty, to see what she knew. "It is true. He has been losing weight for some time," she said.

He was alone that late Sunday afternoon when I visited him. He talked and talked. A pedicure by a qualified podiatrist eleven months before had resulted in an injury. Due to diabetes, the injury had not healed. I urged him to go to the hospital. The next day, perhaps his roomer, a graduate student, who was away that weekend, took him. A new vein, surgically attached, improved the blood circulation to his foot and lower leg and he was sent to intensive care. He recovered enough to be sent to a nursing home and I visited him there in October, prior to my trip to see Cliff and Patti. He expected to go home the next week, but died of pneumonia on October 29 before I returned home. It was weeks before a mutual friend, a fellow pharmacist, told me of his death and service at Amity. "I thought you were responsible for his service being at Amity!" he said.

My fifth grandchild, Auburn Lea Skakle, was born September 10, 1990, at Durham County Hospital. Debbie's pains escalated so quickly that morning that Andy barely got her there. At the hospital, Andy was still afraid he might need to deliver the baby. He was left alone with Debbie and was preparing to put on a white gown when a nurse came in and asked, "Where is the other nurse?"

"I don't know," Andy replied.

Auburn Lea, seven pounds and two ounces, quickly arrived but someone other than Andy was there to receive her.

Three months short of my 65th birthday, in September, I retired from Durham County Hospital Corporation, a second time. I did miss the people and my paycheck, but not the schedule.

Lee came September 21 to attend the Saturday football game with Kentucky; Carolina won 16-12. That evening we attended the UNC Tennis Alumni Lettermen Banquet in the Old Well Room of Carolina Inn. The attention I received from Don's tennis players pleased Lee. Their talking of "Coach" did not bother him. He was not jealous of my receiving pleasure and attention.

During the following week, Lee and I enjoyed the music of the Air Force Band at Chapel Hill High School and visited Wilson Library, where I did research for an article on General Billy Mitchell that I was writing. We went to the New Davis Library for Lee to look for either the book or the videotape of *Lonesome Dove* to share with me; and we attended a lecture by a Russian escapee. Of interest perhaps is that Lee wrote in his journal that I filled my car's gas tank for ten dollars, with gas costing $1.32 a gallon! Was that high then?

There were new developments about the Hatteras property with Phipps' representative, Terrell Smith, and ours, Tim Midgett. They agreed to talk to Mona and me. The Phipps' New York banker, Angelo D. Campanile, agreed to my having the Buxton lot I requested, but the Midgett's lawyer balked at my demand for the oceanfront lot at Hatteras. Earlier the economic downturn had stalled development. Their plans now depended on their favoring our requests and they finally yielded. I received the oceanfront lot I requested and Mona did not need to relocate Hunter Haven. In the settlement, she received that oceanfront lot on which it sat, and another lot, directly across from it. However, if Andy and Eddie were right, I should have asked for additional money, because a part of my lot did not fall under contention.

On Saturday, October 6, I went to Cary to have Andy drive my car and me to the airport for my flight to Massachusetts to visit Beth Skakle, Don's father's 88-year-old widow. I saw baby, Auburn, who was gaining weight and gaining toward the beauty she was to have.

Beth's daughter Paula and husband Bob MacMillan met me at Logan Airport in Boston, to drive me to Beth's Wareham cottage, where Beth spent her summers. We arrived at two o'clock and had a late lunch/early dinner before they left to return to their home in Hudson. It had been 10 years since Ruby and I visited Beth, before our trip to Europe to see the 1980 *Oberammergau Passion Play*. Beth's neighbors' care and concern for her reassured me about her being there alone. *Was I wise to come? Was it too much for my friend to have me visit?*

On Wednesday, October 10, I returned. Andy met me at the airport. I ate supper with the family and arrived at my home sometime after 10 o'clock and Lee called to welcome me home.

The following week, Ruby Lee, Debbie's mother, underwent an angioplasty procedure. I went with Debbie to care for Auburn, while Austin remained at home with his sitters.

Negative feedback from some of Lee's friends and mine made entertain doubts. Shirley Durham asked, "How can you think of marrying a man who is dying?"

His coworker Betty did not want him to leave Kansas City.

On October 17, I met someone at the writer's conference I attended with Elizabeth and John Sherrill at Aqueduct who encouraged me to marry Lee. Ruby from Mississippi said, "Sybil, true love is so rare. If you have six months it will be worth it."

On October 24, I drove to Virginia Beach to spend the night with Beth before flying to Wisconsin to visit Cliff and Patti. Patti met me at the airport, took me to the house, and then returned to work at the beauty salon. I napped and read while Booker and Patti's sister Barb's cat Cinder kept me company. When Cliff came, he and I went to dinner, but hurried back so I could go with Patti to St. James to join her sister Barb and their mother Violet at a Charismatic Meeting of Praise.

Speaking in tongues was normal in that group. Those there seemed to consider it a normal expectation for Christian believers.

I prayed to receive it. It did not happen for me. I believed God would give it at His pleasure.

Spiritual freedom is enough, I thought. *I do not have to have "tongues!" I refuse to be distracted by Satan's attempts to cause me to doubt my salvation!*

Saturday, when Patti and I were decorating for Cliff's birthday party that evening, she mentioned selling the house. Cliff went on the defensive. I did not understand what was going on, but I did not dare press.

We attended Holly Hill Catholic Church on Sunday and the priest's message urged us to love God with all our hearts, minds and spirits. That evening we enjoyed a visit with Patti's family.

When Patti and Cliff and I were together we did not have anything to say to one another. While uncomfortable, I tried to remain relaxed and hoped Christ would prompt conversations and that the Holy Spirit would guard and teach us.

On my last day with my Wisconsin children, Patti cut and styled my hair. Cliff took me to his office to meet his boss, and, while we were there, he wrote a cover letter for my Billy Mitchell article to send to two Milwaukee magazines. On the way to the airport, we talked more than we had all week. "Mom, find someone in Chapel Hill!" he said as he told me goodbye.

Lee had followed through with the dreaded tooth extractions. On October 23, Barb took him to the dental school to have 15 or 16 roots surgically removed during two and one half hours. I had told him, "You have to get your teeth fixed. I will never marry a man without teeth."

Tanya, Beth's younger daughter, met my delayed flight in Norfolk. She and I ate at Wendy's. Then she worked on a school paper and I read until Beth came from work, so the three of us could go to dinner.

On October 31, when I arrived in Manteo, I found Diane and the girls sitting with pumpkins on the front steps of the house. They were excited about their trick-or-treat prospects. Brooke was bubbling, her eyes sparkling. Faye and Snow smiled, while Brooke chattered. It was a sweet moment. Eddie came. Nothing was said about food or how I might fit into their plans. No one offered to take my bags into their house. Too inhibited to be forthright, I said to Eddie, "I will go and spend the night with Myrt." (Wanchese is only four miles south of Manteo.)

"Do what you want to do," he said.

Well, I wrote them of my plans and expected to visit with them, but I did not know what they expected of me. I was not sure they wanted me. I still do not know what they expected me to do.

I tried to contact them by telephone the next day. After several attempts, I drove to Manteo. Their van was parked behind the house. "We just came home," Diane said, but Eddie had left that morning for overnight fishing, so I would not see him again.

I invited Diane and the girls for dinner, but needed to telephone Myrt of my plans. Faye had to connect the phone. No wonder I had been unable to get them on the phone all day.

They chose McDonald's for burgers. When we returned to the house, Faye gave me sheets to make up the couch downstairs and they went to bed. The next morning Diane left with Brooke to take Faye and Snow to school, saying that she did not expect to be back immediately, so I said my goodbyes.

There was nothing to feed the cats or dogs and nothing in the refrigerator. I filled the dog's water bowl and left. I stopped at Hardee's for coffee and a sausage biscuit. I needed to go back to Myrt's to retrieve my prized gold-love-knot earrings Cliff and Patti gave me. Myrt urged me to stay and go to visit one of our cousins.

It was two o'clock before I left for Atlantic Beach and it was seven before I arrived at Peppertree Resort. Lee and I talked three times before Andy and his family arrived around 11 p.m. Lee thought that I may have misunderstood the situation at Eddie's. "Maybe they didn't have money for food," he said.

Surely that was not true. I felt guilty and ashamed. I would have bought food, but their plight was not my fight! What little money I could give would not be enough. Utterly confused by what seemed like unfriendliness, I walked the beach and cried.

The next day, November 6, election-day, incumbent Senator Jessie Helms won in the senatorial elections against Charlotte Mayor Harvey Gantt. Debbie's parents' arrived a little before 4 p.m. It was Ruby and Spencer Coltrain's 42nd wedding anniversary. That evening to celebrate we crossed the bridge from Atlantic Beach to Morehead City to eat at the Sanitary Fish Market, a coastal landmark on Morehead City's waterfront since 1938.

When I returned home on Friday and went to pick up my mail at the post office, I locked my keys in the car and had to call AAA. In the huge accumulation of mail was a letter from a Dr. Gardner from "Insights for Living," who had answered my letter to the Reverend Dr. Chuck Swindoll. His letter of encouragement emphasized the loving, forgiving nature of God.

Journal: *God's love seems more real to me than His wrath. My love for Lee is motivated by compassion, not by lust or infatuation.*

Home again, I was grateful to be in my own bed and back with my friends. When Lee called, he said, "I'm lonely."

When I stopped long enough to feel, I was lonely too.

On November 9, I heard from *The State Magazine.* My article on General Billy Mitchell was scheduled for their December 1991 issue.

Lee arrived November 15 with red carnations. His flight was more than two hours late due to an emergency landing in Nashville, Tennessee. A pregnant woman, traveling with a two- and a three-year-old, had her water break. I did not think women that near delivery dared fly!

On our way home from the airport, I took Lee to see Dr. Crane, a Durham dermatologist, who used liquid nitrogen to remove many ugly, dark, age spots on Lee's face. These would heal while we vacationed a week in the mountains.

We drove to the mountain cottage of Hollow Valley Resort, which I exchanged for a timeshare week, on Sunday. I chided Lee when he could not make the fire burn in the fireplace. I am convinced that he was never a Boy Scout! We took walks. The sun was warm. We sat on the mountainside, overlooking a gorge. He asked me to marry him. "I don't know, Lee. I've not had a confirmation from God."

He chuckled and said, "I asked him and he said it is okay!"

We watched two cavorting baby squirrels, and talked about what we might do if we did marry. Maybe we would buy a condo in retirement community together.

During the week, we visited places near our condo: Seven Devils, where Charles and I had taken a vacation; Mast General Store; the swinging bridge at Grandfather Mountain; and Mount Mitchell.

At eleven o'clock the night before Thanksgiving, Debbie called to tell me that Eddie, Diane, and their girls were coming to them for Thanksgiving, "If you would like to see them," she said.

Yes, I wanted a normal, affectionate relationship with Eddie and his family. Lee and I cut our mountain stay short, packed up the next morning, and drove home to Chapel Hill. That evening we drove to Cary for a family Thanksgiving dinner.

We stopped for a short visit on our way to the airport, November 24, to see relatives of Lee's. He had learned from his cousin Eleanor in Washington, Pennsylvania, that her son George Jr. and his family lived and worked in Raleigh. Meeting George, Kathie and their daughter—their son was visiting his girlfriend in Wisconsin—was a treat. It made me feel our relationship had more substance.

My first Social Security check, for $684, came December 3 and Lee noted that his, $779, was larger than mine. My check was drawn on Don's account. I drew on his until I became 65, when it was refigured and my own earnings were used to arrive at a higher figure, due to the 23 years with Durham County Hospital Corporation. I received 33 dollars from Don's account as part of that benefit.

The day I went to take care of Auburn for Debbie to do shopping, Debbie told me that Diane wanted to go into a business for herself and that she hoped to rent a chalet in Canada over Christmas. This was the only news I received of Eddie and Diane during December.

The Amity UMC choir, directed by Mary Comer presented, "Ring Christmas Bells" and "While Shepherds Watched" on December 16 and I sang with them. Tillie Adams came for a visit. I went with Andy and Debbie to her family's Christmas Eve party in Trinity. We did not get back to Cary and to bed until 3:30 a.m. My flight to Kansas City was at 11:55 a.m.

Lee and Barb met my 3 o'clock afternoon flight Christmas Day. We picked up food, went to his home, exchanged gifts, and ate dinner. While Lee worked as a greeter at a Wal-Mart store, I scrubbed walls and cabinets to remove smoke from an earlier fire and to prepare it for possible sale during my stay.

The house had potential, but needed many repairs, starting with a new roof. A roof requires a big outlay. We cleaned and cleared the basement of broken appliances and made repairs that we could make. I urged him to have his carpet cleaned commercially. One day we did eight loads of laundry at a Laundromat. We washed everything smoke might have touched. I enjoyed helping, but was sometimes too tired to sleep. On my last day, January 4, I insisted we hang the drapes in the living room and in what he called Pam's room before we went to the airport for my flight. It had turned very cold and was spitting snow when we left Lee's house. The Kansas City Airport closed soon after my flight left for Atlanta, where I had a two and one half hour layover.

Andy met me when I finally arrived at RDU and I stayed overnight with his family in Cary so I would be there Saturday to take care of the children for them while they both worked.

On January 10, 1991, I turned sixty-five and became eligible for my own Social Security. Family and friends called and sent cards to wish me well and I received a lovely one from Lee and one from Charles, as well.

January 11, Angela Terez, editor of *The State*, phoned to inform me that "Early Appointment" would appear in their March issue. The next day I gave blood at the Red Cross Center to bring my total to 22 pints, while aiming for two gallons. (I have long since reached that goal and the Red Cross still solicits my O negative blood!)

When Eddie called January 13 to wish me a belated birthday, he gave the bad news that his boat needed repairs again. His degree from Carolina in Physical Education qualified him to teach. Teaching would have given him a steady salary and retirement benefits later. With fishing, his livelihood depended on his boat. He had responsibility for a wife and three little girls! The next day I learned how to wire money and sent what he needed to his account.

The world was watching the situation in Iraq, which was such that President George Bush obtained congressional approval for the "most devastating air assault in history" against military targets in Iraq and Kuwait January 16. He rejected a Soviet-Iraq peace plan for a gradual withdrawal . . . gave Iraq an ultimatum to withdraw from Kuwait . . .

Tanya, my niece Beth's younger daughter, joined the Navy as a reservist, primarily for money for college. With Desert Storm in progress, she was called to active duty to work as a corpsman at one of the Navy clinics in Norfolk, Virginia. The Persian Gulf War would end April 6, 1991.

Irene Burke Harrell's accepted my little poem, "Butterfly," for publication in *Starlight. That* brightened my day.

Mona and Bill came January 24th and we went to Cedar Island to catch the ferry to Ocracoke, and another from Ocracoke to Hatteras, because Bonner Bridge was deemed unsafe for traffic. A dredge crashed into it in October. Our visit was to be a surprise for Jo's 70th birthday. The weather was cold and windy. Carlos had arranged for us to stay at their Sea Gull Motel and when we arrived, he came to check on us. Next morning he left Jo to make her own breakfast to come and take us to Sonny's for ours. When we walked in to surprise her, she was having Irish coffee with a friend Betty Austin. "So, you're the reason Carlos left this morning," she said. "And, why I walked home in the rain last night from the civic meeting, too!"

We celebrated that evening at Breakwater, a newly opened restaurant on the Hatteras waterfront. Jo, dressed in yellow, was a lovely honoree. Jeff, her son, said, "Aunt Sybil, will you give thanks?"

"She's the most religious!" Jo said.

I felt so bad when I heard that the husband and wife who rented Eddie's store space could not meet their expenses and lost the business. Eddie could not return their money, even if he had wanted to do so.

Cliff and Patti in Wisconsin were on a forgiveness retreat that weekend. "It met us at the point of our need," Cliff said.

Gerald Max Stahl, my "boss" for over 20 years, died suddenly March 5, 1991. He had employed me for pharmacy relief the summer of 1967, and requested that I remain as part-time help that fall. I worked for a number of years, some weeks more than 40 hours, without benefits, before I asked to go full time. His death was a great loss. He was a fine man and respected friend.

Lee called March 8 to tell me he had had his ceiling replaced that day and that he planned to get estimates to dismantle the back porch and to have the bedroom ceilings painted. He had asked $43,500 for the house and been offered $39,000. He bargained for an additional $2,000.

When I was with Baby Auburn and Austin that weekend, I found that Auburn was nearly ready to crawl. She was a good baby and Austin was a happy child. I enjoyed my time with them.

When I applied to do more drug screening for Blue Cross-Blue Shield, I got the job, which made it harder and harder to find time for my writing. However, *Potpourri Publications* accepted my little poem, "Eve's Apple," which was Mama's story about having eaten her father's pear, leaving the core on the tree.

Lee wants me to say "we" and for me to sign a card with him to Jo and Carlos. I want to write my own pages. I respect others' opinions but I love them not too much! Every person's outlook is fickle; flawed by prejudices, self-love, and ignorance, just as mine is. I have my own opinions and I form my own conclusions.

My yardman went to commercial properties and Willie Alston came into my life in April, when I needed him most. Alston said he wanted $40.00 to mow my lawn. "I'm sorry, I can only afford to pay $20.00," I responded. "So, good luck to you!"

The doorbell rang. I answered. "Lady, I feel bad," Alston said "I know you a 'ligious' lady and I came from a 'ligious family. I'll mow your lawn for $20.00."

Puzzled momentarily, I laughed and said, "Oh, yes, I do love Jesus." How did he know?

I depended on Willie Alston for many months. I was grateful for his help with my yard and other tasks he performed for me.

Lee asked, "Do you love me as much as you loved Don?"

One person cannot replace another. I replied, "No, I love you as I loved Don, like no one else!"

The second week of May I bewailed that I had not written for a month. Then Irene Harrell accepted "Atonement," a poem, for Starlight. That same week I sent Eddie three thousand dollars to pay taxes to prevent foreclosure on his property. Since my policy was to give to each son similarly, I needed to give a similar amount to the two others. That amount probably was transfers of stock from my portfolio, opened with Don's 40 thousand life insurance payment.

CHAPTER

{ 18 }

When I announced my forthcoming marriage at the church worship service on Sunday before I flew to Kansas City to marry Lee, I asked for prayers for traveling mercies. Our pastor, Rich Vaughan, declared, "Sybil, your announcement shocked me so that I nearly fell out of the pulpit!" He smiled and wished me well.

After my arrival May 9, we began to clear Lee's house. Lee asked Barb to take anything she wanted and tried to reach his stepchildren to invite them to come to take what they would. Then we sold everything that we could, including tools, lawn mower - anything that is part of maintaining a home and a yard. We were unable to sell a nice chest of drawers and could not bring it home with us. Lee gave it to the neighbor who helped us load the truck for the trip back to North Carolina.

We took numerous loads of "stuff" to two or three different charities so little remained when I told Lee, on the night before we were to be married: "Lee, I can't marry you. I'll help you go to an apartment or wherever you want to go, but I just can't marry you."

"Sweetie, what have I done?"

"You haven't done anything. I just can't marry you," I said. "I'll stay and help move you into an apartment."

"I can't stay here," he said, aghast! Poor Lee!

The next morning, I simply wanted to go home to Chapel Hill and to rest. Instead of pressing on to the tasks at hand, we sat down at his kitchen table to do devotions and during that time the pressure between my shoulders lifted and my spirit became quiet. I got up from the table, mixed the rest of the Miracle Grow I had found, and watered what little grass remained in the yard. Neither of us said anything more about our marriage plans.

Realtor John Smith had learned that we planned to marry that afternoon. He came with the final papers for the sale of the house and Lee's check, so that there would not be any misunderstandings about the ownership of proceeds. However, I suspect that our prenuptial, signed and mailed the Monday before, would have protected Lee's assets, as well as mine.

When we went out to find lunch, we rented a Pensky truck for moving, and afterward Lee took me to the beauty salon. The hair stylist was delighted to prepare me for a marriage later that day in Liberty, Missouri.

Barb and her new boyfriend, Mark Adams, awaited us at the chaplain's home, to be our witnesses. Barb had red sweetheart roses for me and a boutonnière for her dad. Before Lee could get parked, he dislodged Chaplain Beasley's mailbox. That cost him an extra 40 dollars for our marriage May 14, 1991.

Lee gave his Ford Econoline van, with 140,000 miles, to The Salvation Army and the next morning we began our exodus to North Carolina in the rented truck, holding the remainder of Lee's household. We had a pleasant, uneventful trip. I drove most of the way. We arrived at my home in Chapel Hill May 17 at 9:30 p.m. and next morning our neighbors Dirk and June Spruyt helped unload the truck.

That evening Lee and I went to Debbie's and Andy's for dinner. Cliff had arrived the day before to attend his father's induction ceremonies into the Intercollegiate Tennis Hall of Fame and Andy had picked him up at the airport. Cliff came home with us that evening and the three of us attended church on Sunday and had lunch at Golden Corral. Uptight and out of sorts due to stress of the week before, I told Cliff I had decided not to go to Athens. "Mom, you deserve to be there!" Cliff said.

Journal: *Perhaps I owe it to Don Skakle and those he taught and coached; to those I watched play tennis and sometimes fed.*

Monday morning Cliff took my car to be serviced. He would fly and Lee and I would go by car. In driving to Athens, Lee and I covered some of the same ground we had crossed the week before. We arrived at a Holiday Inn in Athens, Georgia, and when we told them that we had been married less than a week, they gave us the honeymoon suite.

We missed the press conference luncheon due to my Tuesday morning hair appointment, which the Holiday Inn concierge made for me that morning. That afternoon, Coach Dan Magill of the University of Georgia, invited us to watch the tennis matches from his private box. Cliff arrived while the matches were in progress. The University of South Carolina defeated Georgia for the team championships that year.

That evening, Cliff and I sat at the head table, under a vent, while Lee sat with our friend, Bob Combs, also from North Carolina. Cliff's speech to accept the posthumous honor given his father was the last on the program. "My mother, Sybil, here tonight, was part of all that my father was and shares this honor," he began. Don would have been proud of our son!

Lee and I returned home May 23 and, together in one place to stay, I prayed that Lee and I would be patient and happy with one another as we adapted. However, before we had time to recover, we attended a family wedding Saturday, May 25, at Saint Francis of Assisi Catholic Church in Raleigh. We sat with the bride's grandparents George and Eleanor Kobowchic of Washington, Pennsylvania, and Cousin Charlie Stanley and his wife Mary of Baltimore, Maryland, at dinner. I liked all these Polish kinfolks of Lee.

Lee and I danced in place, for we were celebrating our love and marriage too. He explained to me the tradition of paying a dollar to the bride for a dance and took his turn.

Blue Cross-Blue Shield did not need me the next week. I was grateful for that and that my income tax refund covered Attorney Roy Archbell's bill for January through May 1991. I was suffering with a very painful stiff neck from the sitting under that cold air vent at Athens, and the stress of the last two weeks. I saw my first chiropractor June 4 and again the next day. Rest, ice, and Lee's ministrations helped me get well.

"Bad news travels fast." I heard that Eddie's vehicle had been repossessed that week and that someone had loaned him money to retrieve it.

Lee, a new resident of Orange County and Chapel Hill, had contacts to make. He called Linberger Cancer Center for an appointment, as someone at The National Institute of Health in Kansas City had advised him to do as soon as he could. We went to my bank, State Employees Credit Union, and I signed a spousal consent in the presence of a public notary so that he could have a separate account of his own. Our Social Security checks would go into a combined checking account. With the help of my stockbroker, Lee invested $25,000 thousand dollars from the sale of his house into a personal portfolio.

On Friday, June 7, we took Cole slaw to a picnic at Audrey and Will Heiser's home. Saturday, we were guests at Helen and Bill Peacock's 50th wedding anniversary party. Sunday morning, Lee attended United Methodist men's breakfast. A volcano in Manila, Philippines, threatened the populace June 9, 1991 and the stress and negative feelings made me feel like one - about to erupt!

Mona and Bill offered us the use their cottage. Monday, June 11, Lee and I went to Hatteras. We arrived at 11 p.m. and by the time we unpacked the car and settled in, it was 1 a.m. By the two signs on the store door, we decided that Eddie and Diane had returned to their home in Manteo. One was a sign indicated the store was closed and the other offered an apartment for rent.

We enjoyed our week at Hunter Haven. Being within the sight and sound of the ocean worked its magic for Lee and me. Andy and Debbie and the children arrived Friday. We left to come home June 19 rested, while Andy, Debbie and the children stayed overnight with Diane, Eddie and their girls in Manteo.

At Cary with the children the next weekend, I sent Lee to watch Austin, two years old, while I cooked supper. Lee came back shortly and said, "Austin said he didn't need me. He told me to come into the house."

"You go back out there and watch that baby, Lee!"

Breakthrough magazine accepted my article, "Wake-Up Call," for the June issue and we celebrated Andy's birthday June 24. On the 29th, I invited neighbors for cake and coffee to celebrate Lee's birthday. He was so pleased.

"We can go to your church one Sunday and mine the next," Lee said, when we discussed our worship attendance.

"Lee, I'll go with you to St. Thomas More every week on Saturday, but I cannot miss Amity's services on Sunday."

Lee never joined Amity UMC. However, he attended worship and church school with me and attended the youth class I taught. One of my students asked, "Should we count Mr. Lee?"

"I guess you'd better. If you don't, he won't be counted."

One night as we were engaging in pillow talk, Lee asked, "Sweetie, why did you marry Charles? I was weakening!"

We received an invitation to the christening of my great niece, Stacy Blair Wilson, in Raleigh on July 14 at St. Andrews Presbyterian Church. Her Grandmother Mona and Bill were there, as well as her grandfather, Dr. Virgil Wilson, and his wife Vicky. Stacy's father, Craig Wilson, a Raleigh veterinarian, and her mother Pam were our hosts. Our visit included dinner at their home.

Lee was surprised that he enjoyed the Prayer and Bible Conference at Lake Junaluska, where I took him the third week of July. We learned more about the Apostle Paul, met many nice folks, and had a nice visit and dinner with my friends, Joyce and Tom Dixon, on top of their mountain. The main speaker was Dr. Fred Craddock, Brandy Distinguished Professor of Preaching and New Testament, in the Candler School of Theology at Emory University. One morning, he gave a message on death that especially touched Lee and me. Overall, we had a good week.

Lee and I worked together in the garden that summer and canned nine quarts of tomatoes that our neighbors gave us. In October, Lee discovered my persimmon tree and used a colander to puree enough persimmon pulp for a pudding. Pleased with himself, he pureed an additional half gallon that we froze.

On July 30, while we were grocery shopping, I bumped into Charles. He shook my hand. "I look for you in here all the time," he said. "I want to meet your husband."

I led Charles to where Lee stood at the checkout counter. While they exchanged greetings I drowned in unease. Lee went out ahead with the groceries. Charles followed me outside and asked, "Do you know someone who can help me write my will?"

The following week on Friday, we left to drive to Washington, Pennsylvania, for the 50th Wedding Anniversary celebration of Eleanor and George Kobowchic. I was at the wheel, going the speed limit, on cruise, when Lee tried to reach the cooler in the back seat for sandwiches. We were beyond Winston-Salem, nearing Pilot Mountain. The noise when he hit the gearshift with his knee or foot was deafening. The mechanic at the small town of Pinnacle said, "You've thrown a rod. The engine will need a complete overhaul."

An AAA tow truck came from Mount Airy to pull the car back to the dealership in Durham. Lee and I rode up in the cab with the driver and after we dropped off the car, he kindly drove us to our home.

Lee said, "Sweetie, maybe we should give up the idea of going."

"No! Lee, we can take your car and leave early in the morning and still make it!" I said, remembering the morning Mama fell out of the attic when she went to get her suitcase before she took me to my first year of college. She did not let that dissuade her. Why should the turn of events defeat our plans when we had the car Lee had purchased, a blue Ford sedan?

We arose at 2:30 on Saturday morning and left at 4 to follow our original route. We arrived at the motel in Washington around 2 p.m. and found a bottle of wine from Lee's cousin John Duskey awaiting us. Soon John himself appeared to take us to his home to have coffee with his wife Betty.

The anniversary celebration began at George's and Eleanor's church and dinner followed at Ramada Inn, a lovely affair. When we met Lee's cousin Jean and her husband Jim Swart at the party, Jean insisted that we come and stay with them. We agreed and on Sunday, the four of us visited George and Eleanor on Goat's Hill (Angora Heights), and Cousin Charlie Stanley and wife Mary, who were their guests. We all attended Hillary's Festival at their church where ate pirogi, hot dogs, and cake and played a little bingo. Afterward, Cousin Charlie Stanley took Lee and me to Wolfedale, the area where Lee lived, played, and delivered newspapers as a boy, and then took us back to Jean's and Jim's.

Before we awoke on Monday, Jean had a call from another relative, Stan Duskey. She invited him and his wife Stella to come to breakfast, and Jim baked waffles for all of us. Mary and Charlie Stanley showed up later, and eight of us visited, looked at family photos, and talked until mid-afternoon.

"Lee looks so good," Jean said. I told her about his teeth and our visit to the dermatologist. "You are good for him, Sybil," she said. She told me that Lee spoke of calling Mary, his old girlfriend. Jean had discouraged him and he did not. I felt a twinge of doubt, but dismissed it.

Charlie and Mary invited Lee and me to stop over for a visit with them in Baltimore. We followed them down the mountains of Pennsylvania and West Virginia. With them, we visited The National Aquarium and Baltimore Harbor, and attended Mass at their church. On Thursday, we headed for Virginia Beach and stopped for Chinese food on the way to Beth's home. Beth arrived home from work and Tanya and her friend Robert joined us for supper.

On Friday, we had lunch with my cousin Minerva and her husband Bill, recently diagnosed with prostate cancer. On Saturday morning, we followed Beth to her older daughter Bonnie's home for lunch; and then left Bonnie's for Hatteras. We immediately met heavy traffic. I switched on the radio and heard storm reports, but did not realize we were meeting an exodus of vacationers from the Outer Banks until we reached Bonner Bridge over Oregon Inlet. There was a solid line of evacuees from Hatteras Island. Still, we did not abandon our plans. We had promised to visit Eddie and Diane, who had recently started a new business, which occupied the space Austin's General Store, my father's business, held for 50 years. We continued down the beach, planning to return to Manteo later that evening and to attend the Daniels' Day celebration on Monday, August 18, before returning to Chapel Hill.

CHAPTER 19

Every Saturday, from June through Labor Day, there is a Hatteras community fish fry, with proceeds going on alternate weeks to benefit the Hatteras United Methodist Church and the Hatteras Fire Department, held at the Hatteras Fire Station, located across the road from Eddie and Diane's business. Lee and I arrived in time to eat fish. As we sat on the remodeled store porch to enjoy the fish and fixings, occasional people came by to chat, to confer on the status of the storm and strategies for keeping damage minimal. We looked east toward the ocean and saw a complete rainbow, which delighted us and two of Eddie's young daughters, who sat with us. Rainbows thrill us because we remember God's promise to man after the flood described in Genesis 9; and we remember the fictional pot of gold at the rainbow's foot.

We tarried. Perhaps Bob would not be such a bad storm.

The 57th Daniels' family reunion at Wanchese was scheduled to begin Monday afternoon at four o'clock. We accepted my sister Jo's invitation for Lee and me to wait out the storm at their home, situated beside the Slash. After moderate rain during the evening and night, torrential, wind-driven rain troubled the surface of the

Slash and splashed loudly against the windows of our bedroom. The noise awakened us Sunday morning. The rains stopped for a while and we went to the Hatteras United Methodist Church to attend worship. Visitors outnumbered members.

Sunday afternoon, Carlos took Jo and us down to the lower end of the village, beyond the Hatteras-Ocracoke ferry dock, and beyond the pavement. We hoped to go to the end of the island for a spectacular view of the angry Atlantic surf surging through Hatteras Inlet into Pamlico Sound. We had gone only a short distance before we saw tide breaking through the sand dunes. The raging surf, frothing with foam, battered the shore. Darker gray lines streaked the somber sky as Carlos turned the jeep around to return to dry ground and safety.

Warned, we were not surprised when the lights at the house went off early that evening. Water became a mere trickle from the faucets. The gas-run generator provided lights for a while, but we had no television. The coverage from the battery-run radio was a repeat of earlier reports.

After the generator was turned off, a mantle lamp fed by kerosene provided good light. We visited while we waited for the storm to pass. Jo's and Carlos' sturdy home, with double paned windows and insulation, kept us from hearing the full fury of the wind. We tried to reassure Lee, who lived many years in Kansas City, Missouri, where tornados are the rule.

Water had advanced over the dike, covered the grounds and stood on the second outside step. Lee confessed to feeling both anxious and awed, and both fearful and excited. The house seemed afloat, surrounded by the tidewater. Cowpoke had never seen anything like Hurricane Bob. He was truly frightened, and during the night, he kept getting up to check the water levels.

We had told Lee about the storm of 1936, before hurricanes were given names.

The 1936 storm had been especially violent. Winds gusted up to 100 miles an hour and took the railing and chimney off the old U. S. Weather Bureau. It blew in a window at the top of our stairs, and we ate breakfast with our feet in the water that morning, while the tide rose to the third step of the inside stairway of our home.

Able-bodied men lifted the piano and the kerosene-run refrigerator toward the ceiling, onto wooden-bottle-crate by wooden-bottle-crate. Doors were flung open to let the tide into the house and to reduce the risk of it floating off the blocks, as some homes did during that storm.

A frightened ten-year-old, I watched the tide advance and thought of Noah and the big flood of the Bible story Mama read to me. I was afraid we were to be washed away. As I stood in the middle of an upstairs bedroom, I buried my tear-wet face in the neck ruff of Dobby, our small white dog, and cried and prayed. When I came down the stairs, the tide had lowered.

As the tide receded, a person manned every broom to sweep the remaining silt and water out the doors. The contaminated water in the cisterns, no longer fit for consumption, could only be used to clean the remaining mud and grime from the floors. The smell of tide-wet paper and mold lingered long after the hurricane passed and is still a vivid memory.

Few Hatteras homes had bathrooms in 1936, but tides made the outdoor toilets a hazard. They did not require water for flushing, but their overflow raised the risk of water contamination in the cisterns and the threat of typhoid fever to everyone. Water in the cisterns was unfit for either drinking or bathing. As soon as possible, we needed to pump the water out and clean the cistern, wiping down the interior of the cement structure with full strength chlorine bleach.

Mona and I were 6 and 10 years old. We donned bathing suits and lowered ourselves into the smaller cistern to help with the cleaning. It took much scrubbing, wiping, and rinsing to rid the bottom and sides of the silt that had settled out of the water from the roof of the house. The exhausting work, dirty and tedious, tired us quickly and our older sisters Margie and Jo took over the task.

The American Red Cross provided fresh water, brought over Oregon Inlet by ferry, down the beach over rutted sand tracks, and delivered to us in five-gallon jugs from the back of a large truck. Their service continued as long as needed.

The County Health Department or the Red Cross provided typhoid vaccine to Dr. H. W. Kenfield, our local doctor, to administer to all the residents of the village. After having a first shot, we needed a second two weeks later. We stood in lines on his lawn, outside the door of his small office adjacent to his home, awaiting those dreaded injections.

Refreshing rain did not come immediately in 1936. Dirty clothes accumulated. On a small knoll, higher than most ground in the village, near the Atlantic View Hotel (renamed in recent years), someone put down a pump point. The old dipping vat, where cows and horses, which once roamed free on Hatteras Island, were rounded up periodically and herded through a solution to kill lice and other vermin was the site. The women gathered with their galvanized tubs and buckets, soap, bluing and Red Devil Lye to boil clothes in a tub over an open fire. The hot clothes were transferred into tubs with cold water and scrubbed on washboards. Our mothers worked in the shade of the yaupon bushes on the sandy hill, and we little ones were allowed to spread small items on the bushes to dry.

When the first rain came, Mona and I rushed to put on our swimsuits, to run outside and stand under the water cascading off the un-guttered roof of the theater building next door. Armed with Ivory soap, we yelped and shouted in glee as we lathered and rinsed.

Water is precious. Preserve it! Do not allow dripping faucets and water to run away to waste. Conserve!

Hurricane Bob passed Hatteras Island 40 miles out in the Atlantic Ocean, and the coastal areas of Massachusetts sustained considerable devastation. The wind diminished by bedtime Sunday. We could open windows and let the air dispel the stale, warm interior atmosphere.

By Monday morning, August 19, the water was back in the Pamlico Sound and the Slash where it belonged. The Hatteras United Methodist Church had lost its steeple again. Fresh water flowed freely from the faucets. The deluge of the night before seemed like a dream, except for the debris left by the tide all over the landscape. As Lee and I traveled north, we saw trees uprooted, metal signs crumpled like cardboard from the multiple small tornados that passed through Frisco, five miles north of Hatteras.

As Lee and I left Hatteras that Monday morning, we did not know if we would be able to exit. Traffic was slow. However, we arrived on time for Daniels Day. We took part in the program and I introduced Lee to more of my kin from my mother's side of the family. We ate under the trees of Bethany United Methodist Church, and then we drove to Chapel Hill.

Lee and I were with Andy's children the following weekend. Austin climbed up into Lee's lap, looked up at him and said, "Grandpa, I am so tired," closed his eyes and fell asleep!

I phoned to check on our Skakle relatives in Massachusetts and Maine. All were well. Lee and I declined the invitation to share the week I had given them, a time-share exchange, in Provincetown, Massachusetts, with Andy and his family in September.

The Soviet Union ended in August 1991, and by December 31, the dissolution was final. With a more open and friendly government under Mikhail Sergeyevich Gorbachev, the "Cold War" ended.

Lee and I received an invitation to Kathy and George Kobowchic's 25th Wedding Anniversary celebration on September 20. We got lost, had to depend upon a couple of "angels," two girls who had been painting the clubhouse in Raleigh where the event was held. They led us there. The pig got cooked at 11 p.m. so it did not matter that Lee and I were late arriving.

On Friday, I met Jo and Mona at Southern Pines to do a six Kilometer walk, while Lee stayed at home. Saturday, I cooked the turkey breast to take to a church group dinner party of 12 we would attend at Betty and Earl Allison's house. Sunday afternoon, after church, we attended "Hard Times" by the Playmakers with tickets that Closs and Fred Wardlaw gave us.

October 7, which I always remembered as the anniversary of my father's death in 1962 at 72 years of age, was the day Eddie phoned to request I look for a clarinet for Faye. Lee and I found one in a Durham pawn shop and took it to her the following weekend. We planned to attend the 150th anniversary celebration of the Hatteras United Methodist Church, begun in 1841 and named Southern Episcopal Methodist due to the slavery controversy of the time. The Reverend Fred Roberts, a former pastor, returned to speak at the celebration and we were guests of Jo and Carlos.

We returned to Chapel Hill Monday and on Thursday, we became attendees at *Starbook's* Writers' Conference at Aqueduct Conference Center to talk about books and writing. However, my encounter with a younger, black professor from North Carolina

Central University had the greatest impression on me. Quentine insisted that I *"learn"* to speak in tongues. I thought the Holy Spirit would take over my voice and my will. That it was up to God, not me. Quentine insisted, "It is a choice, like salvation, a matter of surrendering your will!"

"It is the Holy Spirit praying through you," she said.

When I finally allowed my tongue to utter the strange gibberish sounds without trying to figure out what they meant, it was not an overpowering energy. Rather it was like humming a tune without knowing the words. I was still in control. I could refuse. I could surrender my will to God and let the Holy Spirit speak to God for me.

"I will pray with the spirit, and pray with understanding also." -I Corinthians 14:15.

After attending St Thomas More Catholic Church on October 25 at Lee's request, we stopped at Swenson's for a salad and ice cream and at Viking Travel Agency. We were still undecided whether or not we would go to Hawaii; unsure we should spend the $5,000 it would cost, but we picked up a travel book.

Lee and I went to visit Mona and Bill to help Mona celebrate her birthday on November 12. Mona, a home economic graduate of Woman's College of the University of North Carolina, preferred her own cooking and rejected our invitation to dinner at a restaurant in favor of the delicious lunch she cooked for us.

On November 19, Lee and I were at UNC Memorial Hospital from 7:30 a.m. until 3:30 p.m. His tests indicated that the cancer was advancing and Dr. Mohler told us that Lee had nine months to live. He asked him to try a new medicine, to see if it would reduce his pain. Lee, optimistic and philosophical, approached his participation in research of a new medication as an adventure and we began to get our lives in order as Dr. Mohler suggested.

"Lee, I need you financially, emotionally and physically. You can't leave me!" I declared.

"I'm not going to leave you, Baby!" he said. "I am going to fight this thing."

When we saw Dr. Mohler the following Wednesday, he told us that Lee's chest X-ray was normal. Dr Mohler gave Lee a drug named Cumarin, which was not a cure. It was supposed to make Lee more comfortable.

By the beginning of December, he was feeling some better, but we cancelled some of our activities and wondered if we would be able to make the Hawaii trip. We expected Barb and Mark on December 20, so we bought and decorated a tree, my first in five years. It was nice to have Barb and Mark with us and Lee was so pleased, but he did not want them to know his diagnoses. If they knew, they would stay longer. He said, "No!"

On our first visit, Dr. Mohler told Lee, "Mr. Stanley, you will die of prostate cancer. My job is to keep you from knowing how sick you are. Your job is to get your affairs in order and to do what you have always wanted to do."

We did our wills and had them notarized. We had photos made so Barb would have a nice picture of her father. Lee had a small insurance policy on which he had been letting his dividends pay the premiums. When he updated it, he made me his beneficiary instead of his stepchildren.

We thought Hawaii filled the other, the always wanted to do. However, we wavered until Jo and Carlos invited us to help them celebrate their 50th wedding anniversary in Hawaii. We decided we would go, bought two books of six senior coupons for our airline flight, and booked our flight for January 17, 1992.

Then Cliff had a crisis of sorts. Lee said, "Cliff needs us, Honey. We've got to go."

On January 3, we took two of our coupons to fly to Milwaukee to be with Cliff and Patti. On January 5, we attended St. James Church with them and enjoyed the Epiphany music. Afterward, we joined

Gary and Marci Taxman and their family for their son Ethan's bris (circumcision ceremony) at the Jewish synagogue and enjoyed a luncheon buffet provided by the Taxman grandparents.

When we returned home on Monday, January 6, we resumed our preparations for Hawaii, and planned to celebrate my 66th birthday with Andy, Debbie, and the children. Andy and Austin came to Chapel Hill to go to the Carolina basketball game and have dinner beforehand. Austin chattered away while I was cooking supper. He asked, "Grandma, do you like Grandpa?"

"Yes, Austin, he's my sweetie. Do you like Grandpa?"

"Yes, I do," he said emphatically.

When Auburn tried to eat margarine with a fork, Lee suggested she use her spoon.

"She gets less with a fork, Lee!" Debbie observed.

The temperature fell to 15 degrees as we approached our flight date. I called Cliff and he said, "Mom, promise me that when you get to Hawaii you'll stop, slow your pace, and enjoy yourself. Like me, you rush around to get ready and get there, still be in high gear! It's a trait we share."

Dear God, did I teach him that? Poor child! I push until I'm stressed and exhausted. Don did too! Do I get a charge from putting myself through the paces, keeping track of my efficiency and performance, scheduling too much? Please, help us to be more realistic about what we do. Change us where needed, dear Lord.

When I accepted Lee's proposal of marriage, I committed our future and his illness to God's unfathomable love. When we married, even though his cancer had spread from the original site into his bones, we hoped for five years at the least. We prayed for miracles and began to live in the eternity even death does not end.

One evening Lee brought me a bottle of Holy water. "Sweetie, anoint me and cure me," he said.

"I can't cure you, Lee! That's God's department, but I will pray for you."

He sat in a chair by the kitchen table. I wet my forefinger with the water, drew a cross on his forehead with the moisture, and prayed: "To You, O God, nothing is impossible!"

Our car was loaded with luggage, so when we arrived at Cary Debbie drove my car to the airport on January 17. Her mother was with the children. Our flight took us to Greensboro to meet Mona and Bill, who were also going to help Jo and Carlos celebrate. We left there for our seven-hour flight across the United States and the Pacific Ocean a little after four o'clock that afternoon.

How trusting we are, I thought, as we stepped onto the plane. With North Carolina a low 15 degrees, we were happy to be going toward a warmer clime.

We arrived in Honolulu at 8:40 p.m. Pacific time. Mona had made reservations for the four of us at Ashton Waikiki Sunset Hotel. We rented a car and when we arrived at the hotel, the elevator carried us many stories above street level to our suite. We checked our watches. At home in North Carolina, the time was 5 o'clock in the morning. We were very weary, and I felt a bit unsteady. Lee and I slept fine on the pull out sofa bed!

The next morning, before we went sightseeing, we took our luggage to the place where our ship, the *S. S. Independence*, was moored. Since we had a couple of hours to spare, we drove to see the

Pearl Harbor Memorial and watched a film. A boat took us out to a wharf-like landing. "Beneath these waters is a ship - *U.S.S. Arizona* - the tomb for 11,000 Americans."

Back at the ship that afternoon, as we stood in line with leis around our necks, ready to board our ship, Lee said, "I can't believe I've made it."

We embarked at 4:30 p.m. and, after an hour, were assigned to a table with Mona and Bill for our evening meals. We would share the table with the same six or eight other companions for the entire cruise.

At 4 o'clock that morning, Lee awoke in pain. At 6:30, we attended mass in the ship theater. We spent the rest of Sunday at sea.

At the first island, Kona, we stayed aboard ship because Lee was hurting. Nor did we attend the 11:15 p.m. pajama party on January 21. However, we went ashore at Hilo to shop for clothing to attend Johnny Ho Lum's entertainment at 6:30 p.m. the next evening and we started a log for Lee's pain medicine. We knew the codeine in the pills contributed to his tiredness.

Mona volunteered us for the ship's talent show and we decided that we would sing, "It's a Sin to Tell a Lie," a 1952 song written by Billy Mayhew. As we were standing outside a store, refreshing ourselves with cans of soda, we practiced. Bill brandished his can of soda, "You know, someone may think we're singing for money!"

Touring, we missed the afternoon practice with the pianist. We showed up for our performance and the accompanist said, "I don't know that song. You sing it! I'll chord it for you."

After we sang, he said, "I don't think you will be asked to sign any contracts!"

Actually, we would have sung better without his help! Shucks, we never expected to become famous! We knew that we were more audacious than talented from the beginning! Our musical debut memory simply caused us amusement!

One morning, the four of us strung native orchids to make neck leis. We played bingo another afternoon, paid $30 dollars to play and won $76.

Bill and Mona took ukulele lessons and Bill played for the crowd one evening with other students, while I danced with others in the hula chorus line. Mona and Lee were not as daring as we were.

Our scopolamine patches prevented seasickness and enabled us to enjoy the good food. However, one evening at dinner, Lee put his first course of clear soup right back into the bowl. The agitated waiter asked, "Does Mr. Stanley want more soup?"

Someone at our table responded, "Mr. Stanley will not want that soup!"

Lee and I went back to our cabin and Lee said, "Maybe it is my medication!"

Our cruise ended Sunday evening, January 24, and we left the ship in Honolulu at 9 the next morning. Mona and Bill were to stay on in Honolulu for two addition nights to acquire Volksmarching credit before joining Jo and Carlos' party crowd. Their goal was to walk at least one 10-Kilometer walk in each of the 50 United States of America. They achieved that goal and back home the local newspaper did a spread to lauded their success.

Lee and I booked our flight to Kona to join Jo and Carlos, while wishing ourselves at home. Even I felt jaded. When we arrived at Kona, Carlos met us at the airport. The rental cottage was bright and spacious. Other friends were there, and Ken. We took the opportunity of laundry facilities and washed our dirty clothes.

We celebrated Jo's birthday on the 25th and the next day Jo had plans for us to tour the island. We stopped at a grocery store for me to find an antihistamine, for I awoke that morning with a case of hives that had me on fire. (After we were home I discovered the cause of the hives was the "ultra" detergent" I had taken with me and washed my clothes at Kona.)

The road to Saint Benedict, The Painted Church, was narrow and windy. The church sat high on a hill with a cemetery, displaying many white crosses, to the left of it. It had been built 500 years before by missionaries who came to minister to the Hawaiians. They had used the large, colorful murals on the walls of the church to teach the natives the stories of the Bible.

The quietness of Saint Benedict's is a special remembrance. Lee and I sat together on one of the plain, painted benches. We were in God's house. Lee was not doing well, but we were together and God was with us in Hawaii.

Next, we visited the City of Refuge, now a national park. It is located in a setting of palm trees, lava rock, and tidal pools.

We made it through the day, but Lee had nausea and we both fell asleep in the back seat of the car. That evening Jo cooked Lee a boiled egg, but it did not stay down. He was miserable. We needed to be home and decided we would go next day.

The next morning, Carlos called the local airport to learn when we could get a flight to the "Big Island." After breakfast, Jo found me crying on the lovely porch overlooking the Pacific shoreline, across the busy roadway running by the house. Small white boats on cobalt blue water of the Pacific Ocean are part of that vivid emotion-charged time. For the first time, Jo mentioned the time we spent together while our mother was dying, in 1969. She said, "I'd cried and cried when I found she had cancer and was dying. When the time came and you tried to comfort me, I didn't need it."

When Mama took her last breath, I said, "Praise God, it is over!" I turned to find Jo's arms and she brushed me aside. Instead, she turned to a black nurse, and embraced her.

"I'd already grieved so much; shed so many tears," she explained as though she remembered her rejection of me.

Now, twenty-two years later, Jo and I stood on a porch in Kona, Hawaii; Lee and I were flying home to face his death. Perhaps that was the cause for Jo's recall.

As we were leaving, Jo said, "Sybil, I worry about you."

I put my arms around her. She held me and we both cried.

"I know you do, Jo, and I love you so much."

"I love you, Sybil. I'll come and help take care of him if you need me."

"Thanks, Jo. You'd be a better nurse! I'm dreading failure!

"Probably, so," she said.

Jo had a long history of caring for people. Her oldest son Ken, born with a genetic condition, required many operations. Jo, patient and tender, always was there with him. She had been with Daddy when he died. I had stomach flu and was with Mama and Daddy's sister Beatrice (Beattie) in a motel across from Albemarle Hospital in Elizabeth City, North Carolina, when he died in 1962. Jo was alone with him. Yes, she was compassionate and loyal.

We left Kona Monday at 3:35 p.m. on Aloha Airline. Carlos helped us check our bags all the way from Kona; and saw about having the agriculture check. We reached Honolulu in time to take a shuttle to American Airlines and requested standby status on Flight #8, leaving at 6:20 p.m. I wish I had known to ask for special accommodations for Lee. There may have been none. I did not even think to ask!

After sitting up all night on the plane, we reached Fort Worth-Dallas. I asked to borrow a wheelchair from a reluctant attendant. He finally agreed and I wheeled Lee to get something to eat. He ate jelly and toast with juice and I had two biscuits and water. As we ate, Lee snapped at me and I was hurt and angry and smarted from the blow. I cannot remember what Lee said or why it affected me so deeply. He was always gentle, considerate, and never mean. Both of us were stressed and I still faced the ordeal of getting the two of us from one place to another.

Andy met us. While a young woman security officer wheeled Lee to the door, I dashed to a restroom in desperation. Andy took us to his home from the airport. As I started into the house for my car keys, I met Austin coming out, "Where's grandpa?" he asked.

Connie Haas, the sitter, was with the children. Auburn, her eyes bright, came toward me smiling, but we did not tarry long. We stopped to pick up a few groceries on the way home. When we came into the house, the beep of the fire alarm greeted us. I put Lee to bed and left to get items I needed for him and a 9-volt battery for the fire alarm. I picked up our mail at the post office while I was out and Lee fretted that I took too long.

After we ate the dinner, we began an every three-hour medication regimen of Tylenol#3 and Ibuprofen 200mg. He and I napped for 3 hours. Then I found him in the living room and we stayed up until midnight; then slept for 12 straight hours. He never dressed on Wednesday and Thursday. He slept while I did chores - went through mail and paid bills. On Friday, he dressed for the first time since we came home Tuesday. Then on February 1, he slept beyond the three-hour interval and awoke in the morning bright-eyed and alert!

That Sunday, while we stood in the bathtub, I bathed Lee from a warm bucket of water. We both laughed as I poured the warm water over him to rinse away the soap. I dried him quickly and helped him dress. I attended worship while Lee stayed home that day.

The CAT scan on February 3 lasted for an hour and a half. The cancer had spread to the head of the femur bone in his hip joint. We canceled the scheduled MRI. Lee was too tired for anything more.

We saw Dr. Mohler for the last time February 7, when he told Lee that the nausea was part of the disease and that his PSA had doubled in two months. "The tumors are growing rapidly," he said. "Six months, Mr. Stanley, is all you can expect."

Even so, Mohler prescribed EMCYT and said, "It may slow the growth and will make you feel better. It will not cure the cancer."

"You will need Hospice. I will see that someone helps you make arrangements," he said. Before we left the hospital, he saw that we talked to a social worker, who would make the necessary arrangements. We came home disbelieving.

When I was in Eckerd's to get Lee's medicine, I ran into Charles, all dressed up to go to a Valentine's dance. Excited, he bubbled over with talk, but I needed to get water and seltzer for Lee at Food Lion (then in East Gate) and hurried away. As I drove away, I saw him standing on the curb looking back and forth, probably for me. Even as I faced being alone again, I wished him every good and happiness and that he might find someone to share his life, but I did not want it to be me.

Lord, I've been angry today. There have been tears and some tender moments, but mostly I'm angry and I can't blame anyone. I love Lee and would not want him to go it alone, but I am angry. Truthfully, it's irrational; it's probably denial. I don't want to sit and watch Lee sleeping away what life he has left! But he can't help being sleepy with all this medication. I'm tired of picking up used tissues! What a trifle! How will I feel when I am left alone? I won't think about it! It's better to be angry!

"Honey, I'm not going to leave you," Lee said. "I'm going to fight this thing."

Six months was impossible for either of us to acknowledge!

We were to take care of the children on February 8 and 9. I dreaded it without Lee to help me. However, it was diversion. Lee was lying on the couch. Austin wanted him to play. Lee said, "Austin, I don't feel like playing today."

"Grandpa, would you like some water?"

Lee agreed, so Austin went for the water. "Grandpa, do you feel like playing with me now?" he asked.

Yes, the children's need of us and Austin's care for Lee were compensations, but Sunday night Lee moved very slowly. Still, he would not agree for me to call Barb. We had talked of going to see them in Kansas City. We knew now that we never would make that trip together.

On Monday, while I attended the United Methodist Women to fulfill my responsibility as vice president, our pastor came to visit Lee. When I came home, Pastor Rich was sitting on the sofa folding my laundry, talking to Lee. Lee enjoyed their visit. "Next time I will tell him about my baseball aspirations!" he said.

On Tuesday, February 11, I was still able to leave Lee alone. I played Bridge with the University Women's group, but left early to pick up his Emcyt and Compazine suppositories, prescribed for nausea. That evening I gave him Dramamine, which seemed to control his nausea better than the suppository.

I cannot believe as I write this that I entertained Christian Writer's the next day and served them lunch. Lee was not the only one in denial.

Lee still had not agreed, but I felt I could not wait for his approval any longer. I called Barb on February 12 to tell her what was happening here. She and Mark were to go to California on the 14th and to Orlando, Florida, the last of the month. Did I fail to make her understand how sick her father was?

Andy and Austin came by that day and Austin wanted to speak to "Grandpa." That made Lee smile.

Lee fell out of bed the morning of February 16. After a young police office came and put him back in bed, he was there for the rest of the day. Exhausted from the constancy of his needs, I stretched out on the bed beside him that afternoon to recover from my sleep depletion. When Debbie called, I told her that I could not be with the babies. Her mother would take over until I was free again. I needed a leave of absence from all my responsibilities.

Journal: *Lee is discouraged. I am stressed. Taking care of him has a healing effect and I get satisfaction from it. However, when I get too tired and stressed, I begin to resent being in this position. Tonight he said, "Take a gun and shoot me!"*

That would set him free. However much I hate the thought of months of giving him pills, emptying urine, and caring for this shell of a man, I would not want to face guilt and criminal charges. I love him. It surprises me that in spite of the physical limitation of our marriage that I have remained attracted to Lee. His physical presence has been sweet, but I want this phase over. I pray that You, God, will shorten his time of pain.

Andy and Austin, both so handsome, came by after Austin's speech appointment on Monday and Andy replaced a bulb on the front porch. He and Austin took some trash out to the curb for me. Andy and I had coffee. Augustin, the attendant from Hospice, had not come to bathe Lee and I was grateful that Andy was here to help me turn Lee.

That Friday, Mari Szymanski came from Joseph and Kathleen Bryan Alzheimer's Disease Research Center to explain the program and to ask questions before our final decision for cremation. They told me the procedure and what was expected of me.

Journal: *Lee was quiet today. I did not know if it was due to weakness or if he was finding a spiritual dimension, which he and God shared. That night he startled me when he asked that I write to Wal-Mart and obtain an extension to his leave of absence.*

Jo Lowdermilk, my nurse friend from Durham County Hospital days, phoned. When she learned that Lee was ill, she offered to come and help if I needed her.

Margaret Ronman phoned. Sarge Keller requested she call me to tell me his wife Jean Keller had died of cancer. Jean and Sarge and Mike and Don all worked together. The Ronmans and Kellers were neighbors. Margaret said that Jean's funeral would be at St. Thomas More on the 19th. I needed someone to stay with Lee, if I were to go. The Hospice nurse volunteered to find someone for me.

I asked Lee, "Do you know Jesus loves you?"

"Why certainly!"

"Do you know I love you?"

"You bet I do!"

"Old man, drink your milk!"

"Old woman, I don't want it!" he said. He drank it anyway!

I want to love him lavishly, but there are so few ways for me to show him my love other than a little foolish exchange.

My journal also tells another side of my feelings: When *Lee goes home to Heaven I'll be free to write. Until then, I'm chained to pain. No matter! Taking care of him provides an opportunity for me to learn and to serve. I'm at peace. God has been in our marriage in a way I did not anticipate. I have discovered Lee's deep faith. He's not glib with words, but his persona emanates love and acceptance to others. The love and affection my family and friends have expressed regarding him has been a surprise. And I am amazed by the wide circle of friends and family who cherish him. His wealth and treasure are his friendships.*

Lee fell out of bed first thing the morning of February 20, with his head wedged between the side of the bed and the bureau as he lay on his belly. It took two policemen to get him up and back into bed.

Mona phoned later that morning and came from Clemmons to spend a day. Her presence and help encouraged both Lee and me. She helped me rearrange the bedroom to accommodate the hospital bed expected the next day and cleaned out my refrigerator.

A niece from Colorado called and Jean from Washington, Pennsylvania. Mari and Nan from Hospice came that day. When Pastor Rich called, I asked him to wait until the next day to come. When Augustin came, I sent him away.

That evening I called Barb, and Lee tried to talk to her, but was hardly intelligible. When his brother Chet's widow Alice called from California, he did not even try. His rapid decline was startling and the drop in his weight was dramatic as he slipped into withdrawal.

The book about dying that the Hospice nurse gave me explained to me what was happening. When I found him, lying there with his eyes shut and smiling, I longed to know what he saw. Did he see his mother? Did he see others whom he loved before he loved me: his parents, his wives Bobbie and Freda; his brother Chet?

The only time his arms were around me was when I lifted him onto the bedside commode. Then, I held him close and told him that I loved him. He did not respond and how alone and sad I felt!

Barb and Mark made plane reservations for Saturday. Lee slipped into a coma Friday. Friday, I tried to reach a priest and left a message on an answering machine. Having no success, I found my United Methodist Hymnal, opened it to a section with a service of death and Resurrection and read it to him. Sitting by Lee's hospital bed, next to mine, I sang to him and told him how grateful I was for his love and his life. His breathing became steady, without the long pauses. Finally, exhausted and too tired to pray, I stretched out on my bed and put the long night into the care of Jesus and the Holy Spirit. They would pray for me and keep watch until the first light of morning filtered through the beige curtains near the foot of our beds to awake me.

Lee's flesh was alarmingly hot when I touched him Saturday morning and I phoned the Hospice nurse at once. She came immediately and gave me a prescription for long-acting morphine in tablet form, to be given rectally. She said it would enable him to breathe easier. I administered only two doses, one that morning and another twelve hours later.

Mid-morning Saturday, Dirk Spruyt offered to sit with Lee and urged me to take a walk with his wife June and our neighbor Merle. How good the sun on my face and back and the physical exertion in the open air felt!

When Barb and Mark's plane was due, I left Dirk to sit with Lee and went to the airport. We had not discussed how they would get from the airport and I felt I needed to go. Their plane had arrived when I got there. When I could not find them, I inquired at several car rentals. They, in a rental, and I drove up into my driveway about the same time.

Lee's appearance must have shocked them, for his flesh had melted from his body like lard in the sun. He still looked good in December. The picture Barb took of us at the dining table shows us smiling broadly.

The three of us stood by Lee's bed and talked to him as though he might hear us. I think he knew they were with me.

Mark took a nap and Barb and I talked. She told me that she and her father saw one another regularly, even after her parents separated and divorced. "When I saw how happy he and Freda were together, I decided that I needed to accept his divorce from my mother and his marriage to Freda," she said.

That evening for dinner, we ate the delicious roast beef and vegetables Norma Holmes had brought to me. At six o'clock, I finally had a response from Father Kirkpatrick. He explained that he had been meeting emergencies all day long and asked if he could come the following day.

"Please," I said, "I don't think Lee will be alive in the morning."

He promised to be at my house by ten o'clock, after he had completed that which held him. It was eleven before a tall, handsome young man with dark hair and a warm smile arrived. He embraced me as he entered the door and followed me back to the bedroom, where Mark and Barb waited by the high hospital bed. They stood at the foot of Lee's bed. Father Kirkpatrick stood at Lee's head, across the bed from me, to administer the last rites, a simple service of anointing with oil, sanctified by our faith and hope in Christ.

Afterward, we followed the priest to the living room to tell him goodbye and began to prepare for bed. Barb and Mark said goodnight. I promised to call them if anything changed.

I stood by Lee's head, "Honey, the priest granted you peace. Barb and Mark are here with me. I release you to Jesus. Don't stay a minute more than you need to stay."

He took a deep breath, before I had moved from the side of his bed, and was gone. I alerted Barb and Mark.

Lee had willed his body to Bryan Center for Alzheimer's research. His normal brain cells and those from patients with Alzheimer's disease would be compared and studied. I immediately called them, as I had been instructed, and a man arrived quickly from Bryan Center to collect Lee's body.

At 2:30 a.m., I called my pastor to tell him that Lee had died and to request that he perform a memorial service before Barb and Mark's flight in late afternoon that same day. Rich had another obligation in early afternoon, but agreed to a time that would enable Barb and Mark to be here.

As soon as I could, I called my family to tell them of Lee's death and of the plans for a memorial service. Many were too far away to come. Only Mona and Bill and Andy and Debbie were close enough.

When I attended worship that morning, an Amity member came to me with open arms: "Sybil, your witness of faithfulness is a great gift to all of us," he said.

Amity, with my church family, was the best place I could be that Sunday morning, to receive Christ's "words of life" and His comfort. When I returned home, Barb came down the steps, met me on the walk, and embraced me. "You were the best thing that could have happened to my father for this time of his life," she said.

Yes, I believe that. We kept too busy to worry about how sick he was! We lived well the nine months we had, in spite of his impending death. My time with Lee was privileged. During our time together, I learned still more about God's love for us, and we will meet again because God made it possible through the gift of His Son Jesus.

It had been only sixteen days since Dr. Mohler said Lee had six months to live. Ruby of the writer's conference had said, "Sybil, true love is so rare. Even if you have only six months to be with Lee, it will be worth it." It had been nine months.

COWPOKE

He had a penchant for western things-
Horses, cows, cards and art and,
Signed his letters: Cowpoke and
Addressed mine <u>Carolina Moon,</u>
Eight years we corresponded and
Talked by phone for hours, until
Cowpoke corralled Carolina's heart.
His hazel eyes looked into mine
When we finally met
He looked more like Pillsbury's doughboy
with beautiful human hands
Than like big John Wayne, without his boots.
A staunch Democrat, he almost disqualified me
for voting Republican.
He considered me too religious
I thought him irreverent.
We married in Liberty, Missouri May 14, 1991
full of hope in spite of his cancer.
He gave his Ford Econoline to Salvation Army
Rented a Pensky Toyota truck that we filled
With his remaining possessions to drive home
To beautiful North Carolina
For the next nine months we lived life to
its fullest - like it would never end.
January 17, 1992 we flew to Hawaii, that
something we "had always wanted to do."
His illness took its toll and Sunday, January 26
When we toured Kona with family was a sad, bad day.

Cowpoke and Carolina flew home to Raleigh-Durham.
standby, with no hitches, on Monday.
February 7th Dr. Mohler said Cowpoke's time left
with me was now six months instead of nine.

Sixteen days later Cowpoke checked out of our
"bunkhouse" for better quarters in Heaven,
Leaving Carolina Moon alone and lonely.

Epilogue

My desire is to please God and to love beyond my mortal vulnerability. The conflict of the ages, the struggle of every life between good and evil, makes doing that very difficult, something that affects everyone. I have written about many relationships and the years in which those I knew "stalked upon the stage." I often failed to love and they did too. Our selfishness and ignorance kept us from knowing how to love beyond our selves. The duality and duplicity in human nature makes every relationship a challenge, whether it begins with the arrival of a baby or with a new friendship. Living is complex.

Charles met a Durham woman, who was a good match for him. She must have known how to take up for herself. He gave her and engagement ring but they never planned to be married. Sometime she called me to talk about Charles. His typed 1993 note indicates she helped him learn to take responsibility for his anger:

Eva and I came back from a 4-day trip to Myrtle Beach Monday August 29, 1993. It was great as Eva needs stress-release time. Even from me. So, we agreed every time I show impatience, anger the fine will be $5.00 Right! . . . The total fine was $20.00, paid on our return, as I stepped out of Eva's car. We danced at the following casinos... Love as always, Eva and Charles.

Charles suffered from Parkinson's disease, diabetes, hypertension, and coronary artery disease. After he landed in the hospital a second time for overdosing on his regular medications, two of his sons came to take him back to New York. His last letter, hardly legible, came to me a few weeks before his death in a New York nursing home October 20, 1998, as he approached his 77th birthday. Acute heart failure cue to coronary artery disease and diabetes mellitus was listed as cause of death. He had lived more than 10 years since he had open-heart surgery.

I submitted Lee Paul Stanley's "Loyalty" to "American Runs Deep" for publication in *My Folks and the Land of Opportunity* (Pg.169-170). His story follows:

> My grandfather decided to immigrate to America from Poland by way of Austria and Hungary. How bravely they made that journey with a set of twins born in Vienna. Trudging those long miles with small children had to be trying. My daddy and his twin brother were only three years old when they arrived in America at Ellis Island.
>
> The family settled in the industrialized steel mill country of western Pennsylvania. At Washington, Pennsylvania my granddad worked scooping large shovelfuls of coke into the roaring fires of an open hearth. I remember seeing a single line of men clad in heavy aprons and hoods, to protect their shoulders and faces, as they fed the furnaces. Sweating from the extreme heat, each man carried a shovel of coke to add to the blaze. Later Granddad worked in the blacksmith shop. His cheeks were often red from the heat. Thankful for the religious freedom in America, my grandparents seldom complained of their lot or their lack. They built a large two-story house on

Goat Hill and raised four boys and four girls to be loyal Americans.

From boyhood, I recall the unpaved streets; family holiday festivities; and the sweet, sugary, Seckel pears of Washington. Living there was a happy time for me.

My father met my mother in Detroit, where Henry Ford's promise of five dollars a day lured him. However, when his work failed to remain steady, he returned to Washington, with Mom, my brother, and me. My parents opened a grocery store and lunchroom. They served sandwiches, soup and cakes, for which my mom became known, to the men working in nearby steel mills, coal mines, and cattle slaughtering plants.

Dad helped immigrant friends "get the papers" – meaning their naturalization papers – (they) so eagerly sought. Dad also began making smoked sausage. My brother, a year younger, and I, who was ten then, helped by cutting and seasoning about 400 pounds of meat a week.

Dad lost his money, when he was taken (swindled) in an oil-drilling deal. He could not expand his grocery business and lost everything in the Great Depression of the '30s.

My parents taught us to be honest, work hard, have pride, and to love God. I am so happy to have been born and raised in America; so thankful that my grandparents came, impelled by their desire for religious freedom and opportunity of America.

COWPOKE

He had a penchant for western things
Horses, cows, cards and art and,
Signed his letters Cowpoke and
Addressed mine Carolina.
Eight years we corresponded and
Talked by phone for hours until
Cowpoke corralled Carolina's heart
Finally his hazel eyes looked into mine
He looked more like Pillsbury's doughboy
With beautiful human hands
Than like John Wayne without boots
A staunch Democrat he almost disqualified
Me because I vote Republican
He considered me too religious
I thought him irreverent
Yet we married May 14, 1991
By a Liberty, Missouri chaplain
Full of hope in spite of cancer
He gave his Ford Econoline to Salvation Army
Rented a Pensky Toyota truck for us to
Fill with his remaining possessions
We drove to beautiful North Carolina
For the next nine months we lived life
Fully-- like it would never end
January 17, 1992 we flew to Hawaii
Something we "always wanted to do"
Sunday, January 26 a sad bad day
We did a tour of Kona

Cowpoke and Carolina flew home early
On standby on Monday morning
His illness interrupted our plans
February 7th Dr Mohler reduced the time
To six months instead of nine.
Sixteen days later Cowpoke checked out of our
Bunk house for better quarters in Heaven
Leaving Carolina Moon alone and lonely

-Sybil Austin Skakle

Acknowledgements

The telling of the story helped me understand myself and relationships with husbands, friends and kin better than I did when they were happening. In the actual copy editing of the story, my beloved niece, Elizabeth Newton Williams, a copy editor for a newspaper for many years, made corrections, which I in turn made part of the revision. Her comments and questions helped me to flesh out or to eliminate some parts.

Finally, I wanted the opinion of someone less close to me emotionally to read my story. I engaged an associate of a writing group, Peggy Lovelace Ellis, whose vocation is editing. Peggy read my story, found more errors, and made more corrections, which I incorporated.

I am a compulsive editor myself. Reading, I sometimes find, or think I have found, a better way of saying the same thing. Sometimes I decide the location of a paragraph would be better in another place in the narration. As careful as we have been, you may find errors. I was the last to touch it. So, they are mine.

In writing, I attempted to let the actions of the characters tell our story, without moralizing or making explanations. However, the journal entries reveal my feelings. Sometimes you will discover small essays within the body of the story.

The other characters and I grew in the living of these days. We not the persons we were 20 and 30 years ago. I am very proud of the men my three sons have become. Both they and I made mistakes of action and judgment. Life is learning. No bitterness remains because compassion melted away resentments, disappointments, and frustrations. God forgives us, for he knows that we are mortal. He gave us Jesus, His Son, Our Savior.

Eddie said, "It is your memoir, Mom, not mine."

And it is! My story is our history. Do not be offended!

SYNOPSIS OF WHAT CAME NEXT

What Came Next follows another memoir, Valley of the Shadow, by Skakle, The first concerns the death of her husband of 33 years. This memoir tells of her search for another love to replace one lost. Her story includes two love stories. Caught in the values and beliefs of her youth and Bible morality, her values collide with the new culture. She marries Sir Charles. After 5 years, Sir Charles leaves the marriage and she seeks Cowpoke as a confidant. She had never met him person to person but after she and Charles are separated for ten months, she visits Cowpoke, for surprises.

Torn between two human loves and God's love, she seeks to do the impossible, to solve the problem without hurting anyone or compromising her beliefs. The reader may decide the why of the separation and divorce. The author learned much by writing the memoir.

After her divorce, Skakle, cannot decide to remain single and pursue her writing career or to marry Cowpoke, who is dying. When she does marry him, they take a trip to Hawaii. His oncologist had advised him: "Do what you've always wanted to do." The trip was cut short by his illness.

The defense of right to the land, left by her father to his heirs, continues over the ten years and beyond. As a paralegal for her side, Skakle engages with the history of the land that goes as far back as 1711-1712 to the original land grants of Hatteras Banks.